Travel Guide to the World

Providing the essentials to get you the best value and most from your travel experience

Susan Kimmel, MCC

Foreword
by
Rusty Pickett

CORYSTEVENS PUBLISHING
15350 NE Sandy Blvd.
Portland, OR 97230 USA
www.corystevens.com

First Edition, April, 2006

Copyright © 2006 by CoryStevens Publishing

Library of Congress Cataloging-in-Publication Data (on file)

ISBN: 0-942893069

Dedication

Special thanks go to the following persons who made significant contributions to the creation of this book: Jay Kimmel, my husband and travel partner, Margaret Berson, copy editor, Ken Manske, graphic design and technical assistance. Other contributors included Harvey Siamon, Rusty Pickett, Donna O'Neil, Scott Westerman, Bill and Darlene O'Dell. Proofreadings and additional contributions by Emily Kimmel, Julie Westerman, and Joanne Day. For reviews of *Travel Guide to the World* see website at www.corystevens.com.

Printed in the United States of America
CORYSTEVENS PUBLISHING
www.corystevens.com

Contents

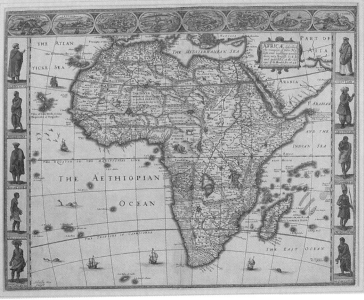

Foreword

As I write this, the great blizzard of 2006 has just rampaged through the Northeast! No doubt, just about everyone in that part of our great nation is thinking to themselves– I should be someplace much warmer and sunnier! They are exactly right, and as a result, the travel industry is booming. Cruise Lines International Association estimates that 12 million people will cruise in calendar year 2006. This is a good thing and a bad thing.

As we baby boomers start to turn 60 this year, more and more supposed 'travel companies' are forming, hoping to allure this affluent market to their Internet marketing sites. They advertise great deals, but may not deliver the value and service that travelers want and demand, let alone any type of personalized service. Additionally, the so-called Internet giants have created the paradigm that they are cheaper–which in many if not most cases is not true.

Susan Kimmel's *Travel Guide to the World* is a compendium of essential information for today's informed traveler. This book provides the reader with a reference source so that the travelers of today can find the best **value** for their vacation adventure, *not just the best price*. With this information you will be able to find a professional travel agent, knowledgeable of today's travel intricacies, ready and able to put together that great "trip of a lifetime!" Relax, enjoy a sip on an "umbrella drink," and start packing!

Rusty Pickett, ECC
Elite Cruise Counsellor
Owner, Shellback Cruises
Charleston, South Carolina
Captain, USN (ret)
Nuclear submarines

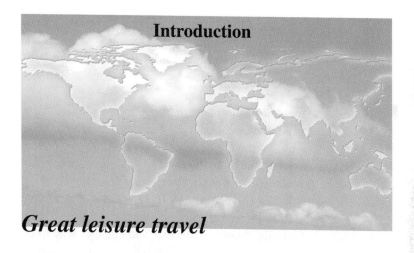

Introduction

Great leisure travel

is about exceeding expectations. The sun rises and sets each day and you may not take the time to notice. However, if you suddenly experience a beautiful sunset after a day of activity on a tropical beach and feel the warm breezes begin to cool as the light slowly fades, your expectations for the moment may be exceeded. Add a great meal, a tropical drink, soft guitar music, perfect service, and the chance to be with others having a great time. Trust your instincts. Your senses will tell you that you are experiencing something unique and exciting and the memories are yours to keep.

Value is what you get.
— Warren Buffett (America's wealthiest investor)

This travel guide is intended to be a valuable reference source for the traveler who wants to actively vacation in many different parts of the world. Ideas are included for destinations, ways to negotiate favorable prices, and how to get what you want as a leisure traveler. There is information on traveling with children, pets, disabilities, and traveling solo or as part of a group. Additional details relate to airline, motor vehicle, train, and cruise ship travel. Extensive references are provided for gathering specific information that can be used to create a vacation plan that leads to the experience you want. In the history of the world, the potential for leisure travel has never been greater. Options and decisions to be made have never been greater. You can venture out based on your own good judgment, or you can acquire some new information from this book that will enhance your next travel vacation.

One of the first questions a leisure traveler may have is, "How do I get what I want at the best price?" The answers tend to be as varied as the people asking the question. A bargain to one person is not the same as a bargain to another and that is a distinct concern of this book. A bargain does not always mean getting the cheapest price. A sophisticated traveler needs to be clear about unique expectations and not simply call around and ask, "Can you beat this price?" Potentially, there is a cheaper and cheaper way to do almost anything to the point of ridiculousness. A major goal of this book is to give suggestions for having a very special and memorable vacation that will likely exceed your travel expectations.

> *Values provide perspective in the best of times*
> *and the worst.* —Charles Garfield

Leisure travel is considered to be the world's largest and fastest-growing business. As employment is re-defined throughout the world because of computerization, labor-saving devices, and technological innovation, leisure activity becomes an increasingly more important element of nearly everyone's life. Employment within the leisure travel industry (all forms of recreational travel, cruises, tours, hotels, restaurants, entertainment, plus vendor services and commodities of every description for the traveler) will continue to prosper with relatively few exceptions. Most people actually contribute in some way to the tourism industry as a part of their occupation, or at least by participating directly in leisure travel activity.

A marked decline in international tourism followed the tragedy of September 11, 2001, in New York City. The U.S. Department of Commerce reports that the number of U.S. tourists traveling outside of the country has returned to pre-9/11 levels and continues to average close to 60 million travelers each year. The World Tourism

Organization (WTO) has projected a steady increase in international tourism and has estimated that gross income for international tourism by 2010 will approach 1.5 trillion dollars.

Special thanks go to two men (Larry Page and Sergey Brin) who formed Google, the world's most popular search engine, and launched their mega-company from a friend's garage in September, 1998. As a result, research of travel destinations and billions of bits of information are far more readily available worldwide on the Internet. Other search engines are also available and the sheer volume of data can be both a blessing and a potential for confusion. More and more travelers are comfortable in navigating electronic information systems, but some get frustrated with promotions that under-report charges, conditions, or may even be fraudulent. A suggested alternative is to consider doing your own preliminary research on the Internet, with travel publications, and then contact a travel consultant with the information you have. At little or no additional cost, you can get the expertise of a professional travel consultant, fully develop your vacation plans, and improve the chances for a great travel experience.

Travelers now have almost limitless options and personal access to vast amounts of information that was simply inconceivable just a few decades ago. John Lennon, for instance, who crafted music about the potential for a world without borders, would likely be struck by the openness of national borders that many people never considered to be possible. Travel to the former Soviet Union and The People's Republic of China now requires little more than a passport and a visitor's visa. John LeCarre, author of many spy thrillers, would have considered it a life-and-death challenge to get past Check-point Charlie in communist-block Berlin. Now, tourists from around the world can visit Berlin, the art treasures of St. Petersburg, the onion-domed basilicas of Moscow, or walk throughout Beijing's Tiananmen Square or Forbidden City, but a tour guide is definitely recommended. The People's Republic of China is making enormous preparations to encourage and to facilitate tourism for the Summer Olympics of 2008 in Beijing.

Airline travel, second only to the private automobile, has become the vehicle of choice for a vast majority of travelers. Ironically, the image of leisure travel now tends to begin soon after getting off the plane, not with the first step outside of your home. The reason for this is relatively simple. Air travel has become commonplace and is the fastest means of getting from point A to point B and back. Passenger aircraft tend to average at least 500 miles per hour once underway. A flight from Los Angeles to Sydney, Australia—a distance of roughly 8,000 miles—is often described as being just three meals and three movies away. You not only get there in less than one day, but are typically pampered with good food, drink, and, in first and business class, seats that tilt back as in a luxury automobile. Cable News Network (CNN), in fact, has reported that there were approximately 4 million "elite flyers" in 2005. The non-luxury coach passengers on international flights will not be able to tilt back quite as far but are generally more comfortable than on domestic U.S. flights. In less than one full day it is now possible to travel more than halfway around the world in relative comfort. On arrival at the final airport the passengers will gather their luggage and pass through immigration and customs. Next, they will start meeting with other people to arrange for transfers, rental cars, cruises, resorts, tours, and the many variations that make up a travel vacation.

Great media attention will continue to be given to the burgeoning population of seniors, boomers, and Generation Xers who are considered prime candidates for leisure travel. The prior generation, who grew up during the Great Depression years, typically worked hard to raise a family and finally retired but rarely went outside of the U.S. Boomers and seniors, in contrast, typically want to see the world and all the best it has to offer within their lifetimes. Incredible options exist right now and everyone who is willing to spend a few dollars on this travel guide will certainly be among the active, frequent, and independent travelers whom the author of this book most wants to encourage and assist. In another context, and in the words of Welsh poet, Dylan Thomas, "Do not go gentle into that good night" – JUST GO.

Prepare for your next travel vacation with enthusiasm. Do your own research and consider the services of a professional travel consultant. Travel with a relish and a flair that only you and your companions can do. Remember to budget for each of the major expenses of transportation, lodging, meals, and entertainment. Allow for hidden expenses such as gifts for loved ones and unexpected emergencies. Even with the best plans, things don't always go as expected. Be prepared for the unexpected and allow yourself to have a great experience.

Leisure travel is largely about making choices and voting. You vote with your dollars and with your feet. If you travel almost exclusively by air, vote also with your "seat." Reward those suppliers and service professionals who provide the services you want and offer the most reasonable prices. Go where the world's receptivity is good, better, and best. Read travel reviews, travel magazines, and books. Consider the specifics of a travel experience that you want and then work out the details and means to accomplish those goals. You are on the right track when you know the experience will be exciting, stimulating, informative, adventuresome, and what you want it to be.

1
Travel Bargains

If you don't get what you want, it's a sign either that you did not seriously want it, or that you tried to bargain over the price.
—Rudyard Kipling

Lowest Price May Be No Bargain

The "magical" way to find bargains, in the opinion of this writer, results from having a clear idea of what you want, detailed search of what is available, a realistic budget, and a fierce determination to get the travel experience you want. The most common reason expressed for vacation travel disappointment results from expecting huge discounts and then receiving far less than expected, or paying a lot more. The world of marketing constantly uses words such as *Discount, Cheap, Free, Bargain,* and *Super Sale* primarily to get your attention. You are led to expect something like fresh strawberries and cream on a chilled plate and you may get a stale fruit bar with artificial flavoring. Leisure travel that gives you what you want and that leaves you with a lifetime of positive memories is not snatched out of the bargain barrel. Getting very good prices and the memorable experience you want is a primary focus of this book.

Watch for the Details

Everyone, or nearly everyone, loves a bargain and the warm-all-over feeling that goes with purchasing something of value for less, or perhaps a lot less, than most others would pay. The "super bargain," however, often neglects significant details, or does not fulfill the buyer's expectations. Personal service is typically the first thing to be cut back or eliminated to create cost savings. An 800-number service may have little or no value in an emergency if there is only a recording, or you do not have all of the data they need. Certain add-on costs (taxes, port charges, cover charges, fees, admission tickets, etc.) are especially frustrating when not expected. Inadequate insurance, or no travel insurance, can seriously disrupt an otherwise great experience. The airport that is a long distance from where you are going may have very high taxi or shuttle costs. A common omission is to not match your personal preferences, lifestyle, and critical needs with what the vendor happens to be selling. The professional travel consultant, working mainly on a commission from travel wholesalers, is likely to provide far more personal service and essential information than the rotating staff at one of the Internet travel companies.

Hot Travel Bargains

Everybody seems to offer bargains. A Google search of the term, "travel bargain," produced over 46 million entries. Consistently finding great travel bargains is part chance, part research, and frequently due to working with a good travel consultant. To get started, it is essential to know your own budget, personal expectations, and what typical costs are before seeking a big discount off the total price. Bargains are mostly about making individual choices between what you consider to be acceptable and what is not. Often, you will find that it is not a matter of calling at random and asking, "Can you beat this price?" You actually need to make some detailed comparisons and match each as completely as possible. A professional travel consultant may be an excellent resource for assisting you to find the best possible value.

A major purpose of this book is to assist you in getting the leisure travel experiences you want, not to dwell on low-cost travel. Many people seem to think that a perfect travel experience can be found at cheap, discount prices with just a little luck. Most of the time, sad to say, the really tempting, red-hot offers are mostly inducements to get your attention. The real purpose is to convince you to pay the under-reported costs in incremental doses. Instead of such a "bait and switch" approach, this book seeks to give you resources and ideas for finding the really good travel experiences that you want.

Compare and Negotiate

Consider hotels similar to properties you have enjoyed in the past. Hotels typically have great variation in availability, size of room, view, location, and other amenities that allow for price adjustment. Each hotel room (or suite) can have up to 40 different prices that relate to supply and demand and marketing factors. If you are shopping for a hotel room, ask for a best price such as AAA, AARP, senior discount, or any promotional specials they may be offering. Ask about the dates for winter rates. If you will be traveling with a large group of people, ask about group rates. One way to create a hotel bargain is to make comparisons of competing hotel rates and be attentive to ways that you can negotiate some element of the room rate. It may be appropriate to ask, "How can I improve on the price?" Ultimately, you may get a less-than-perfect room but the difference in price may be what you wanted. Be polite and persistent about what you want.

Negotiation is a basic skill that is perhaps most prominent when you buy a car or a house, but it can also apply to some elements of travel. Taking the extra time to compare similar offerings will give you a basis for negotiating the stated price. Many sources, for instance, may give you their best price but are reluctant or unable to compare themselves with another source that may be lower. Lowest airfare is one of those examples where the fare may be lowest from the dozens of fares listed on the screen, but there can be large numbers of competing fares that are not part of that website's comparisons. One airline's website is not likely to disclose a better fare at another airline. It takes a combination of creative questioning and actually looking at lots of relevant data to answer a question such as, "What is the best price?" Getting the best price at one source can be very different from getting the best price from all of the potential sources. Sometimes, it is just not worth the time and effort to find the absolute lowest price.

A bargain is something you can't use at a price you can't resist. —Franklin P. Jones

Slightly Off-Season Deals

Consider a winter trip to Europe such as pre-Christmas shopping in Germany, or a "rainy season" British Isles tour where the emphasis will be on interior tours of museums, castles, historic sites, theaters, and concerts. Off-season rates for hotels and nearly all other services will usually be lower and certainly less crowded than during the peak travel seasons. The major difference is that there is much less daylight and the weather may be cold and miserable outside. Creative travelers can emphasize the indoor activities as much as possible. A distinct advantage of off-season travel is that vendors and tourist service personnel usually show greater appreciation for travelers when total numbers are less. Some inconvenience with the weather can translate to big savings. Consider Egyptian pyramids in March as most tourists have left due to rising temperatures. Visit the Taj Mahal in September before the tourist surge in October. Go to New Zealand in March since it is just after the Southern Hemisphere's summer. In Japan, visit the less populated island of Hokkaido instead of Kyoto during the non-winter months. Book the first or last cruise to Alaska for the season. Travel on a holiday, not shortly before or after.

Shoulder Seasons

One of the best ways to experience travel at reduced prices is during the intervals between the high and low seasons. Usually, that means between the winter and summer seasons and is described as the shoulder season. In temperate climates this tends to be during the months of March, April, May, September, and October. The usual rationale is that a majority of people do not want to interrupt their children's school program, or they are attending school themselves. In other instances it is the slightly less predictable times between the dry and rainy seasons such as in the tropics. Hawaii, for example, usually makes great effort to boost tourism during April and May while school is still in session, but rarely needs a boost during the summer, or when it is cold in much of the continental U.S., or during holiday periods. Hawaiian resorts, however, can vary somewhat based on seasons and their location on the leeward (dry) or windward (wet) sides of the island. Ski

16

destinations may be just the opposite. Also, the southern hemisphere will likely be just the opposite. Consult a detailed atlas or perhaps a tourism board for any location to gather information and then consider these favorable-rate times.

> *To sell something, tell a woman it's a bargain,*
> *tell a man it's deductible.* —Earl Wilson

Last-Minute Deals

Bargains are sometimes due to unsold hotel space or cancellations at the last moment. A late check-in at a hotel may create opportunities to negotiate the price, if a room is available. Airlines that predict undersold seats for particular flights may offer those seats to Internet discounters or air consolidators at discount rates. To take advantage of such situations a traveler may need to make a commitment on short notice. The downside of making this your regular bargain-hunter strategy is that if you are obligated to buy an airline ticket at the last moment, you may have to pay a premium price. With airlines cutting back schedules and tending to overbook many flights to ensure maximum occupancy, these last-minute deals become less common.

Out-of-Favor Deals

Consider a destination that has for some reason become suddenly or unexpectedly unpopular. Examples could be a natural disaster, or some other factor that might abruptly interfere with tourism. First, it may be critical to verify that the airport is functioning and that tourist services are available. It is not recommended that travel be considered in areas of major political disruption, or areas that have been declared war zones. Watch for special incentives that are intended to boost tourism for one reason or another. It might be a first-time opening that didn't sell out, a ship reposition (when a cruise ship is being moved from one location to another between seasons), an event that was overshadowed by another, maybe a negative rumor, a high-profile incident in that area, or just some fluke of marketing. These could be additional times to find major discount offers. Consider making it a habit to contemplate how international events in tourist-oriented parts of the world may impact travel for brief periods. Should a few reported cases of avian flu in rural areas of a particular country shut down all tourism to that country? A bargain vacation package could be based on a particular destination simply being out of favor for some reason that is not high risk. Be observant and flexible with your time and doors begin to open.

Selling at a Loss

Travel vendors with millions and perhaps hundreds of millions of dollars invested in their product and/or services typically do not discount their product and their reputation to levels below their true cost. Unsold airline seats, unrented hotel rooms, and unfilled cruise cabins or suites are often a fact of life but generally do not produce the kind of losses that soon puts them out of business. As deadlines approach and as inventory appears to be declining, many vendors will actually raise their prices. Keep in mind that last-minute sales and major discounts usually require full payment at the time of booking and can restrict your ability to make price comparisons, or to change your mind.

It pays to be mindful of the ancient warning notice, *caveat emptor.* It is a time-honored Latin expression that basically means, "Let the buyer beware." Logically, this more-relevant-than-ever advice could be combined with the expression, "If it sounds too good to be true, it probably isn't true." The impersonality of the Internet and the difficulty of resolving problems across state lines or international borders are major temptations for deceitful vendors to exploit consumer confidence. The cautious thing to do is to check your source's credentials before making a purchase commitment. If possible, verify that the offer was not made by a "fly by night" operator.

> *While money doesn't buy love, it puts you in a*
> *great bargaining position.* —Anonymous

Travel Teasers

Would you buy a luxury ocean cruise for $39.95 per day? First, you would want to know exactly what is included with the price. With any offer that appears suspicious, verify all of the terms and conditions. Additional sources for verification could include the cruise line, a state attorney general's office, and basic verification of the seller's credentials. Be wary of any situation that requires an immediate, non-refundable cash deposit to hold the reservation; however, some vendors do require nonrefundable deposits and their service is legitimate. Real vendors with real offers have a history that can be documented and have learned to price their product and/or service in ways that allow them to continue in business. Sometimes vendors offer extra special, time-sensitive deals such as "two for one, kids fly free, kids eat free, or kids stay free." Check to make sure you understand exactly what the offer is and that the vendor is reliable.

Get What You Want, Not What You Asked For

Leisure travel bargains do take effort to find, to negotiate, and they must be relevant to you. The reason that this writer has possibly over-stated the concern about liabilities associated with "bargains" is that huge numbers of consumer complaints are traceable to "bad bargains." "Sticker-shock," however, tends to make bargain-hunters of us all. A leisure vacation is a big investment and *should* provide you with great experiences and positive memories  that are what you wanted. It is the nature of travel marketing, however, to over-embellish the positives and to play down the probable true costs. The suggestion of this writer is that you be cautious, do your own research, and know all of the details. The information provided above is intended to be cautionary and still encourage you as a leisure traveler to "vote with your dollars," and to have a great vacation experience that is what you want and at a realistic price that is disclosed upfront.

Experienced leisure travelers will typically do what they can to avoid paying full resort or cruise brochure prices, hotel rack rates, or premium airline costs. In all probability, however, you will be paying somewhat more than the euphemistic travel ads implied. Experienced leisure travelers can either be a little amused and expect to pay a little or perhaps a lot more than expected, or limit leisure travel to an overly strict budget and perhaps fail to go. Concentrate on the leisure travel experiences that are right for you.

Additional Sources of Information

www.airsaver.com	www.familyonboard.com
www.astanet.com/news	www.fineliving.com
www.bizrate.com	www.independenttraveler.com
www.budgettravelonline.com	www.seniormag.com/travel
www.consumerreports.org	www.sidestep.com
www.consumerworld.org	www.travelbargains.co.uk
www.cruisecritic.com/bargains	www.travellady.com
www.epinions.com/trvl	www.viamagazine.com
www.europe-today.com	www.youngmoney.com/travel

2
Tight-Budget Travel

The most important trip you may take in life is
meeting people halfway. —Henry Boye

The Risk of Being Too Cheap

It is important to be clear about what you actually want from a vacation travel experience, not simply what you ask for. A common dilemma is to search for a hotel in an unfamiliar location based on room price only and then discover that the neighborhood left a lot to be desired, some of the features did not work, you could not check in when expected, and there was a raucous party next door all night long. Likewise, a continental breakfast can be a quick and very low-cost way to start a day of travel if you don't mind putting some cereal and milk in a bowl yourself, pouring your own coffee into a Styrofoam cup, and perhaps adding a muffin, sweet roll, or piece of fruit to your meal. However, if you really wanted to be served a full American breakfast by someone else and have a linen tablecloth, real silverware, and fresh flowers on the table, you may be disappointed with a continental breakfast. A complaint that is often voiced is, "I wasn't very happy. I got what I asked for, not what I wanted."

Kitchenettes Can Be a Great Alternative

Vacation properties may offer some form of kitchen instead of a continental breakfast. There is the possibility of purchasing a few things from a local grocery store. Items purchased from a grocery, such as local residents might use, can be a source for very cost-effective meals and still allow active days of travel. A light breakfast and even a light lunch or dinner can be obvious ways to offset the cost of frequent restaurant meals. Reminder: Not all kitchenettes provide utensils. You may need to confirm what is available for preparing meals, or provide the basics beyond whatever a take-out restaurant might provide.

Travel Light to Keep Costs Down

Fewer pieces of luggage can mean less money in tips every time the bags are handled. Carry-on only bags may facilitate your ability to switch to earlier flights. Shuttles and buses are easier to

use when you have less bulk. You may be less inclined to shop, shop, shop and bring "things" back. Save space with multi-purpose, wash-and-wear types of clothing that can be hand- or machine-washed. Some disposable clothing also may be an option. Light clothing can be layered, if needed, and will ideally dry overnight. The humidity varies in different areas and can significantly impede or accelerate the drying time required. Occasionally a laundromat can also be a great resource. Standard advice is to stay at the laundromat until you are finished. Clothing has a peculiar habit of disappearing just about the time you step outside for whatever reason. It is definitely not cost effective to suddenly have to replace all of the clothing that you just put in the coin-operated washer or dryer. Need snorkel gear or a tuxedo? Consider renting. Need extra casual clothing? Consider souvenir T-shirts that start for as little as three for ten dollars.

A Room with a View

A full ocean view will usually be more expensive than a partial ocean view. A partial ocean view means you can probably see the ocean at certain angles, and that other buildings or trees may obscure the view. Besides, at night waterfront views tend to become extremely dark and tend to be the equivalent of no view at all. At some resort properties a distinction is made between ocean "sides" and garden "sides" rather than views. A clear view of the ocean may be possible only from the top floors that are above the palm trees. Views that are described as "garden, mountain, or city" also vary in price but may start at a lower rate. Watch for the specials that may be in addition to other known discounts (and well below the hotel's top rate, or "rack rate"). Watch for price fluctuations as the economy changes due to any number of different reasons and especially as the seasons change. The change from summer to winter rates can be substantial (unless snow sports are a factor). The in-between times (seasons), often called shoulder rates, will tend to be somewhere between the highs and lows.

The Budget Room Without a View

The clean and safe but older property back from the beach or other tourist attractions may offer even more competitive rates, and the same general factors apply to these smaller properties as well. Why pay for a facility with oodles of amenities unless you fully expect to use them? When traveling with small children it may be possible to get the room rate for two adults and still be able to make adequate provisions for the small children. Verify your questions in advance. An advertisement saying, "Children Stay Free," for instance, often means with existing beds and bedding. In this case, pricing was probably quoted on a per person rate, not a per room rate.

If You Don't Know, Ask

Avoid making assumptions when you travel. If you don't know the price, ask in advance. If you assume you will get a non-smoking room without asking, you may get a very smelly room. If you assume you will get a queen or king-size bed, you may get one or two doubles that are not comfortable. If you assume there will be no additional fees, you can be led to some unpleasant surprises. Using a hotel phone or a marine band phone aboard a ship will be very expensive. Use a cell phone, pay phone, or computer-based options first. Assuming the weather will be good can leave you somewhat unprepared in the event that it is very different from what you expected. It can be a little risky to assume that it will not rain in a "sunny" location. A major one to avoid is assuming that everyone paid the same price. They probably didn't. In some instances the best price may occur at the last moment, but more and more large vendors such as airlines and cruise lines are finding that strategy to be extremely counter-productive. The typical approach now is to offer the best prices from three to six months out, especially if paid in advance or held with a significant deposit, and to offer a credit of some type if the price should fall before final payment. In the meantime, efforts are made to raise prices right up to the departure date and actually require the highest price for those last-minute, "emergency" bookings, or simply let some vacant seats, hotel rooms, or cabins go unsold. The procrastinator, who typically waits until the last minute, is not rewarded and the product (or service) is not depreciated in value simply because it was not sold out in advance. Solution: Ask lots of questions, expect good answers, and do so well in advance.

Playing the Haggle Game

In some countries it is the custom to "bargain" with local street vendors. It becomes a contest between the vendor and the buyer. The vendor wants to earn as much as possible and the buyer wants to pay as little as possible for the product. Most items are not priced and you must ask for the price just to start the barter ritual. Consider an offer from 20 to 30% less than the stated price (asking for 50% off is usually too severe and generally unproductive). Eventually there will either be some "meeting of the minds," or the buyer starts to walk away. The non-verbal act of walking away often prompts the vendor to agree to a little more discount. If unreasonable, simply continue walking away. If the item is not a "must have item," the buyer should have a top price in mind and be willing to walk away if that price is not reached. It is not polite in any country to tantalize a vendor by focusing on an item that you have no intention of purchasing. Also, discounts tend to be better toward the end of the day as the vendor may have to pack up for the day or boost the day's cash proceeds. It likewise tends to help if there are few or no other people attempting to get the vendor's attention at that moment and not reveal the vendor's willingness to take a big discount. Negotiating techniques can be applied to *any vendor* who may have the authority to adjust a price. Seek out people who are in a position to have some control over the price (independent hotels, taxis, clothing merchants, jewelers, and other retailers) and creatively seek more favorable deals.

Travel as a Group and Save

Forming a small or large group of fellow travelers or family members may be a way to share on many expenses to bring the unit cost per person down to an acceptable level. It can also be a way to gain or earn other benefits (known as amenities in the travel industry). Everything from taxis to hotels to cruises may be purchased

at lower rates per person when a small or large group is involved. When traveling, a small group can agree to hire a taxi for the day and have a personal chauffeur to create a special excursion and then pay in cash *at the end of the taxi ride*.

You can potentially negotiate more favorable rates for hotel rooms, cruise cabins, rental cars, and a great many incidentals when a group is involved. You may want to charter a mini-van, a bus, a plane, or an excursion boat, block restaurant space, and perhaps dine family-style. You may be able to block space for private parties, meetings, or ceremonies just for the cost of food and drinks consumed.

Use Public Transportation

City buses, trolleys, and subways can be a great way to get around and view quaint urban areas. The cost is considerably less expensive than what you would pay for a taxicab, but they are not always convenient when you are carrying multiple bags. Backpacks can be a good alternative for day outings but tend to be somewhat difficult to manage in tight areas such as a crowded bus. Shuttles, tour buses, and even water-taxis can also be great ways to get around and see much of an area you are visiting in relative comfort and safety and not spend a lot of cash.

Budget Travel

It can be extremely rewarding to view much of the world's most interesting people, places, and things without paying a premium price to do so. It does take a good bit of creativity and resourcefulness to find reliable vendors of all sorts who acknowledge some willingness to negotiate the going rates. It takes diligence and stamina to find the sources who price their products and services below the market or very competitively in the first place and it frees you from unexpected expenses at every juncture of your travel. The inside cabin on the lowest passenger deck of the least costly cruise line still gets you into the regular dining rooms, buffet, promenade, shows, classes, lounges, theaters, gym, pool, walking or jogging decks, the same itinerary, and the midnight buffet. Be candid with your travel agent or the vendors you contact to structure a budget travel package that can truly exceed your own expectations.

With images of super discount offers being projected by all forms of media, it has become commonplace to think that Internet vendors will come up with the lowest price for comparable products, services, or packages related to travel. Sometimes that will be the case, but to be a valid comparison, all of the essential details must be matched and perhaps confirmed. Example: Prior to Super Bowl XL in Detroit, Michigan (2006), Internet sellers and street vendors had been aggressively offering collectibles, tickets, and associated services. A portion of those offerings were "knock-off" imitations, counterfeit, or just plain unreliable. It is a common error to make a bad purchase of something that was presented as a "bargain." CNN reporters suggested doing business with reliable vendors to the extent possible, paying by credit card, verifying that there is a customer service option available, and verifying the longevity of the vendor (under the same name) when possible. If you have any reason for doubt, why assume that an offer of a major discount is a valid offer? In the field of vacation travel, the professional travel consultant will assist you in dealing with reputable vendors.

Working with a travel consultant may not produce the absolute best, bargain price, but it is one of the ways that disreputable offers are much more likely to be spotted and avoided. Travel consultants carefully follow the trade publications and consistently work with reliable vendors of travel services. This is the person who can usually be contacted directly if something does go wrong. The motto of the American Society of Travel Agents (ASTA) is "Without a travel agent, you're on your own."

Additional Information and Suggestions for Budget Travel
- Consider hostels, small hotels, condos
- Consider inflatable boats (buy, rent)
- Consider motorcycle, dirt bike, ATV rentals
- Consider small, independent car rentals
- Research small, inner-city 2-star and 3-star hotels
- Shop like a local, not like a tourist

Additional Sources of Information

www.amtrak.com	www.freighterworld.com
www.backpackertours.co.uk	www.goplayoutdoors.com
www.backroads.com	www.greyhound.com
www.bizrate.com	www.hostels.com
www.budgethotels.com	www.hostelsclub.com
www.carrentalexpress.com	www.hostelworld.com
www.cheapseats.com	www.megabus.com
www.cosmos.com	www.metropolitanshuttle.com
www.elderhostel.org	www.travelbargains.co.uk
www.eurobike.com	www.trekamerica.com
www.experienceplus.com	www.usarvrentals.com

3
Luxury Travel

*We cannot live for ourselves alone. Our lives are connected by a
thousand invisible threads, and along these sympathetic fibers,
our actions run as causes and return to us as results.*
—Herman Melville

Quality, Variety, Novelty

The emphasis with luxury travel is on the quality of service
and the uniqueness of the product. The number one distinction
between a luxury experience and something less is in the service
received. Being greeted by friendly staff is not uncommon, but
formally dressed staff offering a glass of vintage champagne, fresh
fruit, chilled juice, fresh flowers, and a steamed (or iced) cloth
makes a very pleasant difference and a favorable first impression
compared to "Here's your key. A bellman will show you to your
room, if you like?"

Price Is Not the Main Emphasis

The consumer who wants a luxury experience is not insensitive
to price but is very sensitive to quality and value. The luxury
experience tends to be focused on the anticipated experience. There
should be a high level of service, potential for intellectual
enrichment, newness, gourmet quality food, drink, and all in a great
setting with top quality conveyances from one exciting place to
another. Price is just one of the considerations. The experienced,
luxury-oriented traveler often seeks creative challenges and
refinements on experiences he or she has already had. Air travel
will tend to be first class or business class at agreeable times, and
might include a private jet, float plane, helicopter, or chartered flight.
Travel by car can vary from a luxury-class private vehicle to a
privately chauffeured limousine, a totally equipped motor home, a
deluxe Hummer, or even a basic rental car. On cruise ships it may
mean a move from Holland America to Regent Seven Seas, or from

Oceania to Seabourn, Silverseas, or Crystal. Hotels and resorts selected will provide similar qualities along with great spaciousness, respect for privacy, full services, and great physical settings.

The Pace Is Different

Luxury travel is generally not rushed or pressured. Travel plans tend to be made well in advance and allow the anticipation of knowing exactly where you will be as the seasons change. Great

destinations can be considered at ideal times to fully appreciate the weather, the maximum periods of daylight, activities apart from major crowds, and a non-regimented schedule. Details are often attended to by others and time is likely to lose its harsh sense of urgency.

The Value of the Experience

A different mind-set is generally a part of the luxury experience. The experience itself can be far more relevant than the cost alone. Example: The same party who works diligently to add another percentage point or two to his/her portfolio will sometimes "invest" in front row seats at a professional ball game or entertainment event to savor an experience that cannot be had in any other way. Similarly, the first-class passenger on a commercial jet plane receives exactly the same flight and on the same schedule, but pays much more to receive a different experience than the passengers in coach class. Getting what you personally want usually comes at a premium price and would not be the same experience if limited to major discount shopping only.

All-inclusive Resorts

In direct contrast, the minimalist program that is limited to predominantly buffet dining and house wine is not the luxury package. The luxury all-inclusive is generally much more than being "tagged" with a non-removable plastic wristband that distinguishes you from other guests on a different plan. A luxurious all-inclusive begins with an exceptionally well-located resort with spacious and private living areas, great attention to the common areas, exclusivity of access, attentive service, few *a la carte* disclaimers, and excellence in food, drink, and available activities. Timing would include the prime seasons when weather conditions are not excessively hot or unstable. Activities offered would be extensive and at the least might include golf, tennis, swimming pools, spas, live entertainment, motorized and non-motorized water sports, horseback riding, and options for quiet leisure.

Relating to All of the Little Details

Luxury travel typically implies a seamless connection from one type of comfortable means of transportation to another, assistance with luggage without concern for damage, friendly reception that usually exceeds your expectations, concierge services, and perhaps butler services that are available on request from the moment you arrive and continuing until you depart. Reception may include a complimentary cocktail, hors d'oeuvres, and a drink of your choice, a floral bouquet or fruit basket in your room, vintage wine, or aged liquors. Personal assistance with scheduling activities, meal reservations, and special dietary requests is typical, not the exception. Personal assistance may include activities such as hairstyling, manicure, massage, spa, laundry service, butler service, and responsiveness to personal requests to make the travel experience positively memorable. Another major distinction is that the ratio of total staff to resort residents or cruise ship passengers begins to approximate one-to-one. Guests are not simply left to their own devices unless that is their stated request.

Not a Bunk Bed in a Closet-like Room

Luxury suites are very spacious, private, and often have a large balcony with a great view. Standard amenities tend to include special bedding, a pillow menu, leather furniture, a well-stocked wet bar, and full electronic entertainment centers. They are squeaky clean and well furnished in every respect. Bathroom facilities are similar to what you might find in your own home. Internet connections are commonplace and libraries or reading materials readily available. Spaciousness and mutual respect for each other's privacy would be typical because luxury travelers usually reside in very large homes and are accustomed to a certain level of tranquility for much of their day.

Cruising in Luxury

The following is an overview of cruise lines of special interest to the luxury-oriented American traveler:

• **Crystal Cruise Line** has three ships: Crystal Symphony, Crystal Serenity, and Crystal Harmony. The Harmony is to be replaced by a new ship during 2006. Crystal has been rated as the top luxury cruise line in the world. They have been the winner of Travel & Leisure's reader poll for the world's best large-ship cruise line for the past 10 consecutive years. They are famous for gracious and personalized service that compares very favorably with the world's finest hotels. In addition, they offer great itineraries, excellence in cuisine and entertainment, and overall benefits for their passengers that sets them apart.

• **Silversea Cruise Line** has four ships—Silver Cloud and Silver Wind with 296 guest capacity each, and Silver Shadow and Silver Whisper with 382 guest capacity each. They offer all-inclusive, luxury voyages with comparable excellence of service, cuisine, and overall attractions for their passengers. Their ships are smaller than mid-size and the ratio of passengers to staff is very favorable.

• **Regent Seven Seas Cruises** (formerly Radisson Seven Seas) presently operates five ships as follows: Seven Seas Voyager, Navigator, Mariner, The Paul Gauguin, and Explorer II (Antarctica). These basically mid-sized ships feature creative itineraries and similar excellence to others in the same class.

• **Cunard Lines** boasts the longest history for oceanic cruising and has regal qualities dating back more than 150 years to some of their earlier origins for trans-Atlantic service. Their ships include the Queen Mary II and the Queen Elizabeth II. Sailing with Cunard is a multi-tiered, larger-than-life voyage into time and luxury based on a tradition of excellence. The experience typically focuses on the many onboard amenities and excellence in dining, service, and entertainment.

• **The Yachts of Seabourn** offers somewhat smaller ships that strive to be a leader in luxurious innovations. Cruises are all inclusive and typically include innovative itineraries, fine dining,

alcoholic beverages, excursions, and high quality entertainment on and off the following ships: Seabourn Spirit, Seabourn Pride, and Seabourn Legend. Like Silversea and Regent, voyages include gratuities, complimentary in-suite bar set up, wine with dinner, and non-alcoholic beverages throughout the ship.

• **Windstar Cruises** include WindSong, WindSpirit, WindStar, and WindSurf. The major distinction is that they offer luxurious cruising for the more actively minded who want to experience small ship cruising under billowing white sails and a big taste of adventure with a small number of fellow passengers.

The Luxury Market

The luxury-oriented traveler may blend well with the traveling population at large in many instances. Still, there tends to be real

distinctions that set the affluent traveler apart. For one, it may be the frequency of traveling first class on commercial jetliners, not the occasional upgrade to first class using frequent flyer mileage and/or cash supplements. Cruising tends to be aboard the most outstanding cruise lines and to include the largest staterooms and suites. The most exotic and extensive cruises, such as around South America, Southeast Asia, or even around the world in 120 days, may be selected in place of another Caribbean cruise. Extended stop-overs such as a villa on a private Greek island may be another option. For the affluent traveler the anticipated experience is about comprehensive service, broad satisfactions, and qualitative options. Like the difference between a new Ford or Chevrolet and a new Lincoln, Cadillac, or Jaguar, the real distinction between ordinary and luxury is very much about options and then price.

Luxury travel is the discretionary market for millions of travelers with the means to explore vacation alternatives that are typically well-researched and possibly the dream vacation that is out of reach for the vast majority of travelers. Inspiration for luxury travel often originates with publications such *Conde Nast Traveler* and *National Geographic Traveler.* The experience should rank high on uniqueness, enrichment, excellence in food, beverages, and lodging and also live up to the descriptions provided by travel publications such as those suggested above. In even fewer words, luxury travel is mostly about excellence in service and value received, not the cost. The luxury traveler is more likely than most to be alienated by marketing ploys of any kind that are skimpy on essential details and that lack sensitivity toward them as a person. One of the world's most affluent travelers, Warren Buffett, of Omaha, Nebraska, who seems to have a fondness for luxury air travel, describes his Gulfstream IV-SP jet as "The Indefensible."

Luxury Hawaiian Travel

With record-breaking numbers of visitors to Hawaii in 2005 (7.4 million), there has been a shift in focus. Instead of simply

encouraging large numbers of travelers to come to Hawaii, the focus is more and more on the issues of the quality and value of a Hawaiian vacation. One concern is with protection of the fragile environment and the other is in providing accommodations, cuisine, and activities that are attractive to the more affluent traveler. Also, more focus is being given to preservation of the unique Hawaiian lifestyle for local residents with its rich history and culture that is very distinct from the Caribbean, or South Pacific islands.

The Hawaii Visitors and Convention Bureau (HVCB) and the Hawaii Tourism Authority now openly encourage sophisticated travelers to read reviews of premium resort properties on the various distinctive islands of Hawaii, not just book a hotel. Greater attention is also being given to the expressed different visitor lifestyles. The HVCB has identified their vacation visitors as follows: Avid Travelers, Out-door Recreation Travelers, Culture and Arts Travelers, Golf Travelers, and Romance Travelers. Each group is considered to have specific and refined interests that are not best served by a mass-market approach. For these visitors, the emphasis is on the quality and value of the experience first.

Sources of Additional Information

www.abercrombiekent.com
www.allinclusiveresorts.net
www.all-inclusive-vacations.com
www.breezes.com
www.caribbeanmag.com
www.classicvacations.com
www.cruiseline.co.uk
www.cunard.com
www.destinationhotels.com
www.exclusiveresorts.com
www.iltm.net
www.lhw.com
www.luxuryresorts.com

www.luxurytravelmagazine.com
www.orient-express.com
www.premierhotels.com
www.rssc.com
www.seabourn.com
www.slh.com
www.tauck.com
www.travelwizard.com
www.ultimateresort.com
www.virginisles.com/resorts
www.windstarcruises.com
www.worldsleadingcruiselines.com

4
Destination Ideas

Stop worrying about the potholes in the road and celebrate the journey. —Fitzhugh Milan

All Your Dreams Fulfilled

Leisure travelers tend to have passionate ideas about what they would someday like to see, do, or experience. Each traveler also has a unique mix of personal history, life experience, age, income, and discretionary time. Still, you don't have to wait until the kids are grown up. You don't have to wait for retirement. You don't have to wait until you win the lottery before doing something about your desires, ambitions, and just plain curiosity that is needed for vacation travel. Perhaps you have always wanted to visit a tropical rain forest, the pyramids of Egypt, Stonehenge, a European or Asian relative, an ancestral birthplace, a religious site, or have a scuba diving adventure. Maybe you want to see what Darwin saw on the Galapagos, or the Moi figurehead carvings of Easter Island. The choices and the ideas are all yours. It generally takes a combination of creativity and commitment to reach those goals. After that commitment is made, surprising results can occur. It can be as little as 18 hours, for example, to fly as much as half way around the world. Perhaps something a little closer is what you have been thinking about. The choices are yours to make and the time to plan is now.

The Adventure Traveler

Adventure is described in *The American Heritage Dictionary* as "an undertaking or enterprise of a hazardous nature." It is also described as "an unusual experience or course of events marked by excitement and suspense." These same elements are typical of most completed travel. There is the anticipation, planning, financial commitment, and then the partial uncertainty of exactly how things will go, who you will meet, and what you will do. Often, it is the surprising things that happen along the way and your adaptation to those surprises that makes the best travel memories. It is the challenge of facing new experiences with certain time-management responsibilities and always encountering new people along the way who, in one way or another, are sharing a part of that experience with you.

It does not require extreme physical exertion and life or death risk-taking such as in *Raiders of the Lost Ark* to be a personal adventure. It is getting out and doing, seeing, and tasting things that are not a part of your daily repertoire. The generation that came of age during the Great Depression fought a world war, raised children, and tended to retire without taking time off for travel except for a weekend trip in the family car. The generations that followed, especially today's new seniors, boomers, and their offspring (Generation Xers) see travel not as a privilege, but as an exciting necessity for good health and well-being.

In the words of Mahatma Gandhi (1869-1948), "Live as if to die tomorrow. Learn as if to live forever." The power of his words is not just a reflection of that great icon of Indian independence, but in what you do with the words. Get out and do something challenging that is right for you. Do it with some frequency and commitment, not just the occasional weekend away from the business you are running or the job you are doing. Gliding, hang-gliding, and bungie jumping may be great for some, but not for everyone. White-water rafting, wind-surfing, and parasailing may also be options, but adventure travel can also include a quiet walk on a sandy tropical beach. Adventure for some includes a gourmet meal, a day of sight-seeing, shopping, and actively hanging out with other people at a fascinating new destination. See references at the end of this chapter for additional adventure travel recommendations.

You are what you think. You are what you go for.
You are what you do! –Bob Richards

The Environmental Traveler

Eco Travel is a rapidly growing form of adventure travel for environmentally conscious people of all ages who want to observe Mother Nature up close and experience the endless diversity of different eco-systems. "Birding" (serious bird watching), for instance, is a rapidly growing travel activity as habitats change and the numbers of rare and exotic birds diminish. One of the most exciting recent discoveries reported has been the observation of the Ivory-billed Woodpecker in southeastern Arkansas. It was thought to be extinct for the past 60 years. Perhaps you will see one in its native habitat someday. Additional options include the tropical forests of Belize and Costa Rica, which have become especially attractive for eco-tourism. Another activity for environmentally-conscious travelers that continues to grow in popularity is whale watching. Consider using your travel dollars to contribute to the protection and preservation of threatened habitats and all living creatures. Governments of financially stressed small countries are clearly impressed when travelers from around the world visit to see butterflies, orchids, living coral, tropical sea life, rain-forest birds, manatees, stingrays, alligators, banana trees, natural spices, pineapples, and to view protected habitats from a distance. The Galapagos Islands have had great ecological appeal since being described at length by Charles Darwin, yet there is a real potential for damage by the presence of well-intentioned visitors.

Create and Enhance Your Options

Consider expanding on whatever it is that you already enjoy doing. If your present focus is to do more walking, for example, consider participating in 5K and 10K walking events in your community that may be a financial benefit to a good cause. Possibly go on from there by running or walking in a 26.22-mile marathon, trail hike, or back country backpacking. In the right areas you might seasonally be able to participate in cross-country skiing or novice mountain climbing with a local or regional group of like-minded people. Take a tour with a company that specializes in walking vacations. These tours can include some of the most exotic places in

Some Random Options

African safari
Amateur archaeology
Amateur genealogy
Antiquities tour
Archery
Back country RV
Battlefield tours
Beach combing
Bicycle tour
Birding
Build an icehouse
Camel riding
Camping
Canadian Rockies by rail
Canoeing
Castle, cathedral, and museum tour
Catamaran sailing
Celebrity house tour
Climb a pyramid
Cross-country motorcycle
Deep-sea charter
Dirt-biking
Downhill skiing
Eco tour
Epicurean tours
Fall foliage tour
Float plane tour
Fly fishing
Foliage tours
Go walkabout in the Outback
Golf around the world
Helicopter tour
Hike on a glacier
Hike the Great Wall of China
History tours
Horseback riding
Hot air balloon
Hunting
Kite boarding
Kite flying
Major sporting events
Microbrewery tours
Military history tour

Motor home tour
Mountain bike
Mountain climbing
Mushroom hunting
Music tours
Paddlewheel on the Mississippi
Pan for Yukon gold
Photography
Rainforest expedition
Religious tours
Ride a biplane
River tours
Rock collecting
Run, bike, and swim events
RV off-roading
Scuba diving
Sea kayaking
Snorkeling
Snowboarding
Snowshoe
Spear fishing
Sport fishing
Sports car rally
Stay at an all-inclusive beach resort
Sun, sand, and surf
Surfboarding
Test your survivor's skills
Travel writing
View active volcanoes
Visit Antarctica
Visit with people around the world.
Whale watch
White water rafting
Wildlife tour
Wind surfing
Wine tasting and vineyard tours
Williamsburg, Virginia
Windsor Castle
Yangtze River
Yasawa Islands
Yellowstone National Park
Yosemite National Park
Yukon Territories

the world. Consider taking classes in areas of existing or potential interest at the community college, or with local, special-interest groups and apply some of that energy mentioned by Mahatma Gandhi. An interest in archaeology or world history, for instance, has limitless possibilities and it is far more meaningful to visit actual sites and perhaps meet with people who have developed sustained interests in those topics. Likewise, cultural tourism can include tracing the history of art, music, architecture, and all of the creative arts and sciences back to some of their origins. Visit Leonardo da Vinci's Florence and Milan, or pick up on the trail of Dan Brown's *The DaVinci Code*. Visit the battlefields at Normandy, Verdun, and Agincourt.

Go Where the Fish Are

Fly fishing on a remote lake. Sport fishing in the Sea of Cortes. Deep-sea fishing in the South Pacific. Trout fishing on a mountain stream. Halibut fishing off the coast of Homer, Alaska. Wild salmon fishing on the Columbia River. Spear fishing off the western coast of Florida. Sturgeon fishing on the Willamette River below the Oregon City Falls. Scuba diving with an underwater camera off the Great Barrier Reef of Australia. Troll for Pike on the Great Lakes. Capture piranha in the Amazon River. Crabbing off the coast of Maine. Go by charter boat, by pontoon plane, a rafting trip, or simply fish off the dock.

Athletic Travel

Activities are virtually unlimited and both structured and unstructured tours are available throughout much of the world. With good hiking boots, a backpack, compass (maybe a GPS device), all-weather gear, and determination, the road is open to your imagination. Athletic activities can be combined with group tours, possible competitions, and either attending sporting events as a spectator or as a participant. Options, at a minimum, may include climbing, hiking, biking, gliding, hang gliding, kayaking, diving, canoeing, four-wheeling, wave running, water skiing, snow boarding, sailing, and all athletic games. The serious amateur or professional athlete who trains for an Olympic event may work out daily and enter many competitions but will have just one chance each four years to compete for Olympic Gold and must travel to get to those events. Travel has long been a necessity to participate in athletic activities of one's choosing. A marathon, for instance, may attract thousands of participants but the observers, well-wishers, and officials will represent thousands more. For each very active sports participant there tends to be a very high number of spectators who likewise need to consider travel periodically to get away from the easy chair and television. Play-offs and championship events are likewise major opportunities for travel. Take your personal athletic interest to the next level.

Gourmet Travel

Many people travel to enjoy the world's diversity of cuisines. Most travel is associated with the consumption of exciting new foods in exciting new places. You don't have to be a professional cook or nutritionist to enjoy the "epicurean delights" that are available in all parts of the world that are different from home cooking and the neighborhood fast-food eateries and restaurants in your home town. The sheer pleasure of learning more about cooking, baking, desserts, hors d'oeuvres, wine tasting, salads, dressings, sauces, fruits, spices, herbs, and vegetables can be an insatiable quest. As just a minimum summary of possibilities, different styles of cooking can include Cajun, Burmese, Chinese, Thai, Indian, Italian, Viennese, Dutch, English, Irish, Southern [American], New England style, Kosher, Tropical, Latin, African, Polynesian, Aussie, Russian, Polish, Danish, French, Swiss, Greek, Turkish, Middle Eastern, and a great many more. Restaurants of every type can be found throughout the world that cater to travelers. There are also the possibilities of traveling to a cooking school in France, Italy, or a destination of your choice.

Options for the Group Traveler

Group travel generally takes substantial effort to get started and coordinated but often has special qualities for building lasting relationships and can reduce travel costs. Examples would include a family reunion, a sports team, square dancers, quilters, military reunions, and possible groups as follows: collectors, religious, wedding, alumni, theater, seniors, singles, fitness, jazz lovers, history buffs, weight-loss groups, bridge players, occupational groups, writers, students, sports, adventure, clubs or organizations, big band music, mystery lovers, poker players, extended or multi-generational families, and essentially any kindred spirit group with at least one specific interest in common. A travel consultant or a "pied piper" (group recruiter) can help to form the group. Once established, there is good potential for saving money at group travel rates. Friendly group interaction also adds many positives to the travel experience. A musical theme could include Big Band music, jazz, classical, rock n' roll, celebrity performers, or any musical period up to the present. Variations could also include any topic that will help to form the nucleus of a group. Form a group in conjunction with your travel agent and many benefits can accrue.

Sources of Additional Information

www.adv-cycling.org/tours
www.adventures-abroad.com
www.adventuresports.com
www.adventuretravel.com
www.adventuretraveltips.com
www.adventurewomen.com
www.african-safari.com
www.alaskawildland.com
www.americanhiking.org
www.austinlehman.com
www.away.com/ideas
www.backcountrygear.com
www.biznettravel.blogs.com
www.budgetexpeditions.com
www.concierge.com/travelideas
www.earthwatch.org
www.eldertreks.com
www.ethnicgourmet.com
www.europeanexplorer.com
www.fieldandtrek.com
www.fodors.com
www.gapadventures.com
www.gorp.away.com

www.lovingyou.com
www.military.com/travel
www.militaryconnections.com/reunions
www.militaryliving.com
www.momsminivan.com
www.mtsobek.com
www.napsnet.com/travel
www.newsday.com/travel
www.realadventures.com
www.rei.com
www.responsibletravel.com
www.see.america.org/travelideas
www.tgv.com/EN_ideas
www.theromantic.com
www.travel.dicovery.com/ideas
www.travelandtransitions.com
www.uktravel.com
www.walkingsoftly.com
www.walkingvacations.com
www.wherewillwego.com

Checklist of Places to See or Things to Do

Suggestion: Circle the following that you seriously want to visit within your lifetime. Then go back and prioritize your top ten "must visit" choices ranging from one to ten with number one representing the highest priority.

Abu Dhabi, UAE	Chesapeake Bay
Acapulco	Chichen-Itza, Yucatan
Acropolis, Athens	Colorado
Adirondack Mountains	Copper Canyon
Alaska	Costa Rica
Alhambra	Crete
Alligator Alley	Denali National Park
Amazon River	Disneyland
Amsterdam, Netherlands	Disney World
Anastasi pueblos	Dixie
Angkor Watt	Dracula's Castle, Romania
Antarctica	Easter Island
Arc de Triomphe	Edinburgh, Scotland
Ardennes Forest	Eiffel Tower, Paris
Australia	Empress Hotel, Victoria
Ayers Rock	Ephesus
Baja	Fiji
Bali	Galapagos
Bavaria	Gallipoli
Beijing Olympics	Gibraltar
Belize	Giza Pyramid
Bering Sea	Glacier National Park
Black Forest	Grand Canyon
Black Hills	Great Barrier Reef
Blue Danube	Great Wall of China
Bora Bora	Hagia Sophia, Istanbul
Brandenburg Gate, Germany	Havana
Branson	Hermitage, St Petersburg
British Columbia	Hong Kong
Budapest	Iceland
Burgundy	Indonesia
Cairo	Ireland
Canadian Rockies	Jerusalem
Cape Canaveral	Kakadu National Park
Casa Blanca	Kangaroo Island
Cayman Islands	Katmandu
Champs Elysees	Kauai

Kenya	Nashville	Shangri La
Key West	Negril, Jamaica	Silk Road
Khyber Pass	Nepal	Singapore
Kiev	New Zealand	South Pacific
Kilimanjaro National Park	Niagara Falls	Stingray City
Kuala Lumpur	Nile River	Stonehenge
La Pravda	Normandy	Straits of Juan de Fuca
Lake Geneva	North Carolina	Suez Canal
Lake Titicaca	Oahu	Swiss Alps
Lewis & Clark Trail	Oktoberfest	Sydney Harbor
Lincoln Memorial	Oregon Trail	Tahiti
Lisbon	Orient Express	Taj Mahal
Lisbon Antigua	Outer Banks	Tasmania
Little Big Horn	Oxford	Tenochtitlan
London	Palace of Knossos	The Louvre, France
Luxor	Panama Canal	The Road to Hana
Machu Picchu	Parthenon	Three Gorges Dam, China
Madagascar	Patagonia	Tibet
Madeira Island	Pearl Harbor	Timbuktu
Madrid	Quebec	Tower of Pisa
Malacca	Red Square	Trinidad
Malta	Rhodes	Turtle Island
Mardi Gras	Rio de Janeiro	Tuscany
Marquesas Islands	Roatan, Honduras	Vail
Mekong Delta	Rocky Mountains	Vancouver Island
Mexico	Roman Coliseum	Vatican
Milford Sound	Samoa	Vicksburg
Monaco	San Francisco Bay	Victoria Falls
Monte Video	San Juan Islands	Viking Museum, Oslo
Monterey Jazz Festival	San Juan, Puerto Rico	Waikiki Beach
Mount Fuji	Saxony	Wales
Mount Kenya Safari	SeaWorld	Whale watching
Mozart's Vienna	Seychelles Islands	White Cliffs of Dover
Nantucket, MA.	Shanghai	

Next, prioritize your top three choices and start
taking specific steps to accomplish your travel goals.

International Destinations to Consider

Canadian Provinces

Alberta	Newfoundland	Prince Edward Island
British Columbia	Quebec	Northwest Territories
Labrador	Nova Scotia	Saskatchewan
Manitoba	Nunavut	Yukon Territories
New Brunswick	Ontario	

Central America

Costa Rica	Mexico	Yucatan
El Salvador	Nicaragua	
Guatemala	Panama	

Caribbean/Gulf of Mexico/Mid-Atlantic

Agile	Haiti	St. Maarten
Antigua	Jamaica	St. Martin
Aruba	Martinique	St. Vincent
Bahamas	Montserrat	Trinidad & Tobago
Barbados	Netherlands Ant.	Turks & Caicos
Cayman Islands	Puerto Rico	Virgin Is. (U.S.: St. Thomas,
Cuba	San Andres	St. John & St. Croix)
Dominica	St. Barts	Virgin Is. (UK: Virgin
Dominican Rep.	St. Kitts	Gorda, Tortola, & others)
Granada	St. Lucia	

South America & Antarctica

Brazil	Paraguay	Falkland Islands
Chile	Argentina	Galapagos
Ecuador	Uruguay	Easter Island

Western Europe, Atlantic, and Mediterranean

Azores Islands	England	Netherlands
Austria	France	Portugal
Belgium	Germany	Scotland
Bosnia	Ireland	Serbia
Herzegovina	Italy	Sicily
Canary Islands	Luxembourg	Spain
Crete	Madeira Islands	Switzerland
Croatia	Malta	Wales
Czech Republic	Monaco	
Cyprus	Morocco	

International Destinations to Consider

Northern Europe
Denmark	Latvia	Norway
Estonia	Lichtenstein	Sweden
Finland	Lithuania	

Eastern Europe
Armenia	Poland	Turkey
Bulgaria	Romania	Ukraine
Greece	Russia	
Hungary	Slovenia	

Middle East
Abu Dhabi	Lebanon	Oman
Dubai	Israel	Qatar
Jordan	Kuwait	

Additional African Continent & Vicinity
South Africa	Uganda
KenyaTanzania	Madagascar
Rwanda	Egypt

India & Southeast Asia
Myanmar	Vietnam	Bali
Thailand	Borneo	Malaysia
Cambodia	Java	

South Pacific & Central Pacific
Australia	New Zealand
Cook Islands	Fiji Islands

Eastern Asia
China	Okinawa
Taiwan	Japan
The Philippines	

Explore the United States as You Explore the World
State Travel Directory:

Alabama .... www.touralabama.org
Alaska .... www.travelalaska.com
Arizona .... www.arizonaguide.com
Arkansas .... www.arkansas.com
California .... www.visitcalifornia.com
Colorado .... www.colorado.com
Connecticut .... www.ctbound.org
Delaware .... www.visitdelaware.com
Florida .... www.flausa.com
Georgia .... www.georgiaonmymind.org
Hawaii .... www.gohawaii.com
Idaho .... www.visitid.org
Illinois .... www.enjoyillinois.com
Indiana .... www.enjoyindiana.com
Iowa .... www.traveliowa.com
Kansas .... www.travelks.com
Kentucky .... www.kentuckytourism.com
Louisiana .... www.louisianatravel.com
Maine .... www.visitmaine.com
Maryland .... www.mdisfun.org
Massachusetts .... www.mass-vacation.com
Michigan .... www.michigan.org
Minnesota .... www.exploreminnesota.com
Mississippi .... www.visitmississippi.org
Missouri .... www.visitmo.com
Montana .... www.visitmt.com
Nebraska .... www.visitnebraska.org
Nevada .... www.travelnevada.com
New Hampshire .... www.visitnh.gov
New Jersey .... www.visitnj.org
New Mexico .... www.newmexico.org
New York .... www.iloveny.com
No. Carolina .... www.visitnc.com
No. Dakota .... www.ndtourism.com
Ohio .... www.ohiotourism.com
Oklahoma .... www.travelok.com
Oregon .... www.traveloregon.com
Pennsylvania .... www.visitpa.com
Rhode Island .... www.visitrhodeisland.com
So. Carolina .... www.travelsc.com
South Dakota .... www.travelsd.com
Tennessee .... www.tnvacation.com
Texas .... www.traveltex.com
Utah .... www.travel-vermont.com
Vermont .... www.visit-vermont.com
Virginia .... www.virginia.org
Washington .... www.tourism.wa.gov
West Virginia .... www.westvirginia.com
Wisconsin .... www.travelwisconsin.com
Wyoming .... www.wyomingtourism.org

5
Travel Tips

If you reject the food, ignore the customs, fear the religion and avoid the people, you might better stay at home.

—James A. Michener

Vacation Travel Tips

Travel tips have a lot in common with stock market tips—once the subject is mentioned, nearly everyone has their own personal recommendations. Internet travel websites are typically loaded with implications that everyone who responds to their travel blasts will have a great experience. The key issue, in this writer's opinion, is to sort through the vast amounts of travel information available and then carefully research those details that are most likely to meet your preferences and budget. The chances are very good that someone else's travel experience would be distinctly different from your own.

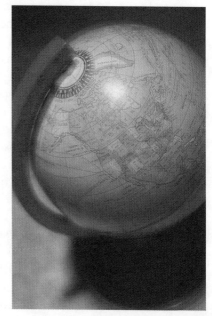

It often takes detailed research and planning to match up personal preferences to create a great travel experience. Choices alone can be somewhat overwhelming. There are in excess of 5,000 hotels in the cities of London and Paris. A quick Google search for the Westbury Hotel in London, a 4+ star property in the heart of the Mayfair District starting at approximately $275 per night/per person, could produce a very different hotel by the same name that starts at $108 per night/per person. In other instances, a property with a great reputation based on word of mouth may now have an entirely new management and price. The quaint property with the traditional, Olde English décor may now be ultra-modern and lacking in any character that would tell you what city you are in once the door to the room is closed. Keeping up-to-date and matching traveler's preferences for budget, location, and other factors is performed by area-specific travel professionals all of the time. A quick search of the Internet alone cannot do the same thing.

Ideas to Discourage Bad Things from Happening

Before starting on a vacation trip, ask a neighbor, friend, or relative if they will periodically observe the exterior of your residence and pick up packages or newspapers while you are away. You can request a delivery hold on the mail and newspaper, but an unexpected package sitting outside your door for days projects the image that no one is at home. Be extra cautious about disclosing details about your vacation plans except for the very few who need to know. It can also be a good precaution to use an office address, post office box number, or cell phone number on your luggage identification tags. This can prevent a possible burglar from getting your actual address as you are in transit to the airport, or just waiting in line to check your bags. Consider securing your residence with a monitored alarm system. Double-check window locks and stops, take extra precautions with doors, and possibly leave a radio or television on with a slightly subdued volume to further discourage a possible intruder during your absence. Electric timers to turn lights on and off at pre-set times can be very helpful. Set up a mutual house watch with a trusted neighbor. Protecting personal identification from intruders is now more important than protecting basic family possessions.

Anticipate Extra Expenses

All-inclusive resorts may sound very romantic and imply that virtually everything is pre-paid. However, on closer inspection, that is sometimes not the case. Gourmet restaurants within the

plan may add surcharges to the menu selections for all-inclusive guests. This can be especially true for out-of-season seafood such as Dungeness crab, lobster, premium cuts of meat, vintage wines, expensive liquors, and assorted delicacies. Alcohol and wine may be limited in both quantity and quality with a surcharge for premium selections. Sometimes, the bar will put up a sign that says only one drink per person at a time. In other words, you cannot order a tray full of drinks and walk off with it. Also, three meals a day or unlimited opportunities to drink and eat are not always included. There are variations such as the Modified European Plan (MEU). Under the Modified European Plan only two meals per day are available. You are typically on your own for the other meal. If you are extremely active and depart early or stay out late you may miss even the two meals that were prepaid. Often, all-inclusive plans will charge extra for horseback riding, scuba diving, and motorized activities such as wave-runners, powered boats, motorcycles, power scooters, golf carts, and green fees. Potential extra costs are typically a matter of choice and are not as troublesome when you can anticipate the choices in advance, not by surprise. Resorts like Club Med, Sandals, and Beaches all have optional extra charges; especially for items such as scuba diving and motorized water sports.

Guarding Plastic Money

A friend just had her purse stolen from a shopping cart while at the grocery store. Suddenly, she had no money, no credit card, no identification, no keys, no cell phone, and her dog was locked in the car! The theft had occurred in approximately 1-2 seconds. Fortunately, the store manager assisted with a temporary cash loan and helped to get the dog out of the car. A traveler could likewise

be very vulnerable if all identification, credit, and cash was suddenly stolen. Suggested solution: Carry two different credit cards and photo IDs in separate, secure places. Consider setting a low cap limit on one of the cards. A low level of credit approval helps to prevent a credit card thief from running up a huge balance that can be very difficult to get settled to everyone's satisfaction. Other plans are also available. Watch credit card receipts that display all of the credit card numbers and expiration date. In such instances, simply cross out all but the last four digits of the card and then sign. Also, not all establishments will accept particular credit cards. To conserve cash be sure to ask first if your type of credit card will be accepted or not. One alternative is to have an American Express card that may be accepted where others are not. Creatively conceal these few critical documents to prevent any surprise loss and have a back-up system in case one set is lost for any reason.

Credit card companies offer card protection in case of loss or theft. It can be worthwhile to check into the specifics of your plan well in advance. If not satisfied with the protection plan, consider changing credit card companies. At the very least, keep a separate copy of the card details and the phone numbers to contact in case of a problem. Keep one copy away from the actual card(s) and consider leaving another copy at home or with a trusted adult. In some instances, a credit card may not be accepted but a traveler's check will be. There may be a small fee for using a traveler's check but they are safer than cash. And for tipping and trivial amounts where a credit card is not appropriate, keep a supply of one-dollar bills that is likewise kept in a pocket or place separate from your ID and plastic money.

Shop Where the Locals Shop

Convenience stores often charge high market prices for much of their inventory. Airport vendors, like movie theater vendors, are noted for high prices. The solution, where time allows, is to identify the grocery stores, pharmacies, and other vendors that the local residents are most likely to use. It may be worth the fare to ask a taxi driver to take you to a supermarket or department store nearby. Check the local newspaper to get the names of such places that are catering to the local residents, not the one-time-only tourist. At some destinations, it may be possible to purchase bottled alcohol at major discounts. Some cruise lines allow passengers to bring alcohol on board as long as they consume it in their cabin. Other cruise lines will hold alcohol until a passenger disembarks at the end of the voyage, or a corkage fee may be charged to have the alcohol served at your table. Check with the cruise line or your travel agent to be sure of the rules before you leave on your trip.

Getting All Charged Up About Dead Batteries

Batteries have unpredictable lives and often frustrate you when needed the most to take a one-time-only photograph, make a cell phone call, or to use your laptop computer. The alternative is to carry extra batteries or a charging unit with you. Often, you may need an adaptor that allows you to convert from 220 volts to 110 volts and recharge a battery. These are typically very small and easy to carry but very hard to find when you do not bring them with you.

Required Documents

Domestic travel passengers age 16 and above must have at least one government-issued identification with their recent photo. Passengers traveling internationally must also have a valid passport. Current exceptions for U.S. citizens include Bermuda, Canada, the Caribbean, Mexico, and Panama. The only documents required

for those countries for air and sea travel through 2006 will be a certified birth certificate and government-issued photo identification. Land crossings in those countries will allow a certified birth certificate only through 2007. International security trends, however, suggest that a valid passport will soon be required for all U.S. citizens to travel to any international destination. Recommendation: Go to a local post office and inquire about a passport.

Children Crossing Borders Alone

Children under age 16 traveling from the U.S. to Canada (or under 18 for Mexico) who are traveling alone, or with only one parent or guardian may be required to present a notarized letter of consent from the absent parent(s). If both parents are present but one of the minor children has a different last name, it may be necessary to present a certified birth certificate (not a photocopy), not a passport. A sample consent form can be found at www.lawdepot.com. Check under "other forms." Also, it may be helpful to check with the airline's website, or www.travel.state.gov/travel/documents.html.

Broaden Your Business Skills

Research the possibilities for on-the-road business opportunities to supplement whatever it is that you usually do as a career. Perhaps you can be a professional photographer on the road, or maybe a guest lecturer in your business field. Another option is to acquire knowledge that would be of interest to some specific group. Perhaps you are already part of a mobile actor's group, a musical group, or writer's group. Consider the ways that you or your group might entertain, consult with, or train others in another city, or country. It may be possible to attend a seminar, school, university, or other training site in a different area to upgrade your skills and to make new business contacts. Pre-arrange to tour comparable businesses in the area of your choice to learn what works well in their business (examples: hotels, restaurants, retailers, wholesalers, or virtually any other product or service). Utilize your accountant's services in advance to develop a business/ travel plan that will meet the IRS test for being actual business activity and not simply a vacation. A major issue is to document the relationship between the travel and your business. Build a detailed paper trail of your activities, your contacts, your housing, transportation, meals, and the positive results that can be attributed from your business travel.

Keep written information strictly for your accountant. If possible, tie in your activities with a training conference in the area of your choice by surfing the web and using your own employment resources. Family members may have to be excluded from the tax deduction. Be sure to consult with your personal accountant well in advance. Focus on what works the best in other parts of the world. Get a jump on how products and services are brought to the marketplace, marketed, and the changing technology involved. It is little surprise that markets are now mostly global and consumers are more and more international. You may be, or in the future may be, more of a business traveler than you imagined.

Additional Sources of Information:

- *The Tightwad Gazette* by Amy Dacyczyn
- *Secrets of Six-Figure Women* by Barbara Stanny
- Fodor's Travel books
- Lonely Planet guidebooks
- Rick Steves' Europe
- Footprint Travel Guides

www.1000traveltips.org
www.2ontario.com/traveltips
www.abcsmallbiz.com
www.activitiesforkids.com
www.adventuretraveltips.com
www.aphis.usda.gov/travel
www.asiatraveltips.com
www.bbc.co.uk/holiday/tips
www.bti-worldwide.com
www.btnmag.com/businesstravel
www.budgettravelonline.com
www.businessknowhow.com
www.businesstown.com/travel
www.businesstravel.about.com
www.cdc.gov/travel
www.concierge.com
www.entrepreneur.com/travel
www.fabuloustravel.com/tips/tips
www.familytravelguides.com/tips
www.forbes.com/lifestyle/travel
www.foreignborn.com/study
www.freeliving.com

www.freetraveltips.com
www.geopilgrim.com
www.getlostbooks.com
www.inc.com/magazine
www.langhoff.com/tips
www.lizweston.com
www.msnbc.msn.com/id
    6559150
www.nbta.org
www.nfib.com
www.smartmoney.com/travel
www.state.gov/travel
www.stretcher.com
www.taxreductioninstitute.com
www.travelchinaguide.com
www.travelsmith.com
www.traveltip.org
www.travelwriters.com
www.tsa.gov
www.unclefed.com
www.webfoot.com/travel/tips
www.womentraveltips.com

6
Special Occasions

Kites rise highest against the wind,
not with it. —Winston Churchill

Wedding Anniversary Travel

Travel may actually be one of the most memorable ways to celebrate a wedding anniversary (and possibly an opportunity to renew wedding vows). This very special moment is much more like the honeymoon than the wedding ceremony itself and not uncommon to be celebrated as a couple rather than as a group of friends and relatives. With an entire world to choose from, one of the most ideal travel vacations for an especially memorable anniversary is the all-inclusive resort hotel property, or cruise ship. Either of these settings is likewise ideal for exchanging an anniversary gift.

Honeymoon Destinations

The top non-U.S. honeymoon destinations recently identified by CNN Money Magazine (2005) were as follows:

- Italy (Florence, Rome)
- Fiji Islands
- France (Paris)
- Tahiti (Bora Bora)
- Caribbean (St. Lucia and others)
- Mexico (coastal resort areas)
- Australia (Sydney)

Recommendations for honeymoon destinations within the continental United States favor areas with good access for family and friends and include high-profile areas such as:

- Palm Springs/LA/Anaheim
- Washington, D.C.
- San Diego
- Las Vegas
- DisneyWorld, Orlando
- Miami, Key West
- Boston/New York City
- San Francisco
- Lake Tahoe, Reno
- Phoenix, Tucson
- Charlestown, SC

The public information center of the Chicago Public Library has compiled the following list of both modern and traditional wedding anniversary gifts by year. The traditional gift is placed in parentheses.

1st	Clock (paper)	28th	Orchids
2nd	China (cotton)	29th	Furniture
3rd	Crystal, Glass (leather)	30th	Diamond (pearl)
4th	Appliances (linen, silk)	31st	Timepiece
5th	Silverware (wood)	32nd	Conveyance (car)
6th	Wooden (iron)	33rd	Amethyst
7th	Desk set (wool, copper)	34th	Opal
8th	Linens, lace (bronze)	35th	Jade
9th	Leather (pottery, china)	36th	Bone china
10th	Diamond (tin, aluminum)	37th	Alabaster
11th	Jewelry (steel)	38th	Beryl
12th	Pearl (gemstone)	39th	Lace
13th	Cloth, fur (lace)	40th	Ruby
14th	Gold (ivory)	41st	Land
15th	Watch (crystal)	42nd	Real Estate
16th	Silverware	43rd	Travel
17th	Furniture	44th	Food
18th	Porcelain	45th	Sapphire
19th	Bronze	46th	Original poem
20th	Platinum (china)	47th	Book
21st	Brass, nickel	48th	Optical device
22nd	Copper	49th	Luxury item
23rd	Silver	50th	Gold
24th	Musical instrument	55th	Emerald
25th	Sterling silver (silver)	60th	Diamond
26th	Original art	75th	Diamond/gold
27th	Sculpture		

Recommendations for honeymoon destinations outside of the continental United States include the following:
- Caribbean (St. Lucia, Turks & Caicos, St. Thomas)
- The Bahamas
- Costa Rica
- Hawaii (Big Island, Oahu, Kauai, Maui)
- Fiji (great exchange rate, no tipping)

- Mexico (especially coastal resorts)
- Canada
- Sandals Resorts
- Beaches Resorts
- Club Med Resorts
- Most Cruise ships

Holiday Travel

A cruise can be an excellent holiday experience that can readily include extended family, friends, and be a great means of reaching out to make new friends who are sharing the same holiday. Example: Carnival Cruise Line, the world's largest, offers many very reasonable packages. The trick is to book as far in advance as possible to ensure the cruise and destinations that your group wants. Likewise, if there is a land destination that could enrich your holiday experience, make a hotel/resort reservation far enough in advance to ensure the room category you want and the dates you want. Often the biggest issue is to be sufficiently assertive to get ahead of the big crowds that are common during the holiday season. If not driving to your destination, you will need to make airline reservations at the earliest possible time and for the same reasons. Thinking like a "pro" is not a designation that you earn for being a *procrastinator.* Additional options can be to watch for holiday specials and book early for best price and/or selection, or schedule air travel on the actual holiday, which has far less volume than the dates immediately surrounding the holidays.

Travel for Health Reasons

The objective of travel will sometimes be more for necessity than for recreation or business. Healthcare prices have been increasing far more rapidly than most incomes and more rapidly than any other major service in the United States. One alternative that deserves *very careful* research is medical treatment in other parts of the world. Minor example: At one time doctors recommended that asthma patients move to Phoenix to reduce pollen exposure. The eventual problem was that incoming residents wanted all of the flowering trees and plants that could be cultivated in the new area and soon the pollen count was as high as in the cities they had left. The standard disclaimer is that before making a decision to seek health care outside of the United States, research the alternatives in great detail and in full consultation with your treating physician. Don't rely on anecdotal information and keep in mind that legal remedies in another country may be impractical. In a global world it is no longer inappropriate to at least consider international healthcare.

Family Reunion

If someone else in the family is not already working on a reunion plan, consider working on one yourself. Once started there is typically a desire to repeat the experience on a regular basis such as every five years and as new family members are born, married, graduating, and moving on in years. You can feel the camaraderie and warm feelings in spite of the effort to set it up the first time. You will likely be able to take advantage of group rates on hotels, cruises, meals, transportation, and other activities. There will be opportunities for group photos, sharing at mealtimes, and the chance for different generations to mingle and to get better acquainted. The really hard part is getting started. A professional travel agent could help you to put the family puzzle pieces together.

Graduation

Recognition of special accomplishment is always appropriate. Spending some carefree moments away from school demands  can be a very beneficial experience before doing what it takes to enter the world of work. Graduation dates are generally definite and certain and known enough in advance to do careful vacation planning. For some people it can be a special incentive for graduating on schedule. For others it may make more sense to be a surprise reward for actual accomplishment rather than increased pressure to perform. A vacation trip before starting a new job also solves the dilemma of asking for time off within the first year or so of new employment.

Retirement Celebration

Like the graduation reward mentioned above, retirement is typically something that is contemplated well in advance and deserves special recognition as one of life's major accomplishments. It may also signal a major change in lifestyle and distinct new allocations of time and effort. On retiring from a career as a teacher, this writer received a satirical card that said, "I don't know what I'm going to do when I get up in the morning and by noon I'm not even half done." Every major lifestyle change deserves some time in a neutral and pleasant environment to think through some of those new priorities and new ways of doing things. Make the experience special. Make it a memorable celebration to mark the beginning of a new way of life. As my celebration, on the actual day that school started for another year, I was enjoying the sand and surf on a small island in Banderas Bay, Puerto Vallarta, Mexico, and I went parasailing!

Special Birthdays and Anniversaries

All birthdays are important, but as we become adults, it is the birthdays that end with a zero that tend to get the most attention. Zeros signify that another decade has passed and a new decade is ahead. These are anticipated occasions that deserve special recognition in the form of doing things that are not a part of the everyday routine. Celebrating with travel on the actual birth date may place you out of sync with the holiday travelers and therefore be even more special. Birthdays and anniversaries can both be ideal occasions for vacation travel. It may be that your parents (or grandparents) are approaching a 50th wedding anniversary. It could be an excellent time to encourage family members to pitch in and pay all of the travel expenses to make the "50th" a very special occasion.

Divorce Getaway

One of life's events for approximately 50% of the married population that may or may not call for celebration is the finalization of a divorce. Chances are that it will be a very different kind of celebration but something that does deserve space and contemplation "of the rest of your life" in a positive setting of your choice. It can be a time to consider implementing a personal plan that does not require the coordination with and acquiescence of a marital partner. Consider Hawaii, the Bahamas, or the Caribbean. Consider a Carnival cruise Fun Ship with great activities on board and many excursions to choose from at each port of call.

Special Achievement Recognition

A specific reward in the form of a travel vacation could be for a job promotion, completion of a project, acknowledgement of community service, retirement, or a multitude of life's events that deserves special attention. It doesn't have to be winning of the Nobel Peace Prize, or even winning of the lottery. Vacation travel can be a very rewarding experience and a time to be away from the day-to-day details that lead to a particular accomplishment. Life is short, consider travel.

Additional Sources of Information

www.boomersabroad.com
www.divorcemag.com
www.doublenickels.com
www.familyreuniontravel.com
www.growinglifestyle.com
www.holiday.com
www.honeymoons.about.com
www.honeymoontravel.com
www.retirementtravel.com
www.retirementwithapurpose.com
www.thebigday.com
www.travelhealth.com
www.travelsense.org/tips/holidaytravel
www.treatmentchoices.co.uk
www.vacations.specialoccasiontravel.com

7
Travel by Private Vehicle

*The car trip can draw the family together, as it was in the days
before television when parents and children actually
talked to each other.* —Andrew H. Malcolm

Economy for the Whole Family

The Travel Industry Association of America reports that up to
85% of all domestic summer vacations are taken by car, or some
form of recreational vehicle. The primary motivation for planning
a road vacation with the family vehicle of choice is usually based
on including the whole family, all travel accessories, and maybe
the family pet(s) at the lowest possible cost. This may be very true
for younger families on tight budgets and especially with smaller
children or infants that can be a real challenge in big crowds, long
lines, extremely confined spaces, and unfamiliar surroundings.

Whether it is a short trip to grandma's house for the holidays,
a trip to Yellowstone, or a trip across the country, the personal
vehicle is going to be economical. You probably will not have to
pay taxi or parking lot fees, airplane fares, inflated cost of airport
food and drink, shuttle fares, or rental car costs on arrival and then
cruise costs, hotel costs, and major restaurant costs versus the small,
roadside motel with a kitchenette that allows preparation of most
or all meals for the family with your own groceries. A car is the
way to go for lower cost and convenience. Other travel options
can still be reserved for long distances and situations where a
personal vehicle is impractical.

Scenic Travel vs. Speed of Travel

Another major factor is the time factor. Driving eight hours
per day usually averages about 400 to 500 miles per day and can
result in the cost for three meals per day, plus daily lodging costs,
gasoline, and related car expenses. This can add up to quite a bit
over many days, and nights, on the road. Eventually, it can make

more sense to do the quick flight in a matter of hours rather than be out on the highway for days and weeks to reach the same destination.

Another factor that is often underestimated is the potential for a mechanical breakdown that must be resolved quickly and perhaps under very difficult circumstances. Sometimes a very time-consuming tow by a wrecker may be required before repairs can even begin. In some instances it may be beneficial to organize a caravan of two or more vehicles that will assist each other as needed and provide a more diversified group experience to the vacation experience. One or more motor homes can be another alternative that can add creature comforts and reduce the cost of roadside lodging in exchange for high acquisition cost and high fuel cost. Among the obvious motor home amenities are the ability to make scenic stops at will, cook, clean, sleep in your own bed, and have a convenient, private bathroom.

Parking, however, can be somewhat more difficult and likely requires staying at an RV park to get electrical power and to empty

 holding tanks, replenish water supplies, and drop off accumulated garbage. Roadside breakdowns with a motor home, travel trailer, or fifth-wheel trailer can be proportionately more expensive to correct than with a personal car or SUV. Still, the open road beckons to all who hear the call.

Vehicle Accessories to Consider
Being out on the highway with the family requires a higher level of self-sufficiency than a commute across town. Items to consider include good maps (possible GPS), working flashlights, road flares, a back-up battery that is fully charged, a few hand tools for minor emergencies (especially for safely changing a tire), extra

wiper blades, an emergency kit that you make up in addition to the simple kits sold at auto parts stores, blankets, food, water, jumper cables, neck pillows, and select personal items. A cooler plus can opener and bottle opener can also be very helpful. Four-wheel-drive vehicles may be great for changing weather conditions, towing purposes, and off-road adventures, but they may not be enough to cross a snowy mountain pass. Chains may be required. Under severe weather conditions, especially high in the mountains, there could be temporary road closures. Commercial, over-the-road truckers were once advised by some companies to carry the correct change to make a public telephone call in the case of an emergency. Now, a similar recommendation for travelers on the highway would be to carry a cell phone. Reception, however, can be poor or non-existent in remote areas. Be sure to check with your cell phone company to confirm areas of reception. It may also be appropriate to check on possible roaming charges.

Leisure Boat Travel

Small boat travel is an increasing source of recreation or vacation travel based on the steadily increasing ownership of personal boats in the U.S. and Canada. The United States Coast Guard reports that there are approximately 70 million recreational boats in the U.S. alone. Such small boats also represent a greater risk of injury or accident than is typical of most road trips. Small boats have more unpredictability while boarding and de-boarding because of wind, waves, current, and other differences. Balance and agility are more important on floating docks, ramps, and slick surfaces of the boat itself. The risk of capsizing, sinking, collision, or other accident such as a bilge-area fire, or getting lost in the fog also tends to be worthy of consideration. Experience (and Coast Guard rules) has shown that there should be at least one approved life vest for each passenger and crew member. Running lights should be readily visible for evening travel. Also, navigational gear, a possible radio for salt water or very large lakes, good charts, and navigation updates should be available. A marine band radio can be especially valuable and a source of getting local weather reports and contribute to the success of a water vacation on your own. Additional water vacation options can include water taxis, ferryboats, river cruising, sternwheel cruising, glass bottom boats, sea kayaks, jet boats, catamarans, sailboats, inflatables, and virtually anything that will float on water. Three-fourths of the earth's surface is covered by water. On-the-water travel possibilities are unlimited.

On a recent Star Princess cruise, a guest nautical lecturer, Dave Drummond, described his voyage on the Intercoastal Waterway (ICW) in a 27-foot sailboat with a special 3.5-foot keel from Lake Okeechobee, Florida, to New York Harbor without ever being in the Atlantic Ocean. Perhaps you would like to sail among the beautiful islands of the eastern Adriatic from Dubrovnik to Opatija. There could also be great possibilities for sailing in the Caribbean and Mediterranean.

Additional Sources of Information

http://maps.yahoo.com	www.hertz.com
www.aaa.com	www.historic66.com
www.alamo.com	www.koakampgrounds.com
www.arizonahighways.com	www.mapquest.com
www.autogolfspain.com	www.mauirentacar.com
www.avis.com	www.national.com
www.backroads.com	www.oars.com
www.bestofalaskatravel.com	www.packyourgear.com
www.budget.com	www.route66.com
www.dollar.com	www.thefloridakeys.com/
www.enterprise.com	houseboats
www.eurocar.com	www.thrifty.com
www.familytravelgames.com	www.us-101.com
www.gpscity.com	www.yellowstoneparknet.com
www.hertz.co.uk	www.yellowstonevacations.com

8
Airline Travel

The Bird of Time has but a little way to fly—and lo!
The Bird is on the wing. —Omar Khayyam, *Rubaiyat*

Vacation Air vs. Cheap Air

Finding cheap airfare to get from Point A to Point B and then back home again is a common strategy. Here is what you might expect: few if any frills, possibly awkward scheduling, extra stops, peculiar routes, a coach class seat, a fully loaded plane, and in return you get a cheap airline ticket. Sometimes everything runs smoothly and you get back and forth as quickly as expected. In the case of severe delays or missed flights, the high cost of extra meals or lodging could quickly eat up gains from the discounted airfare.

Vacation air is different. In planning a vacation, you have a choice. You can either purchase airline tickets separately, or you can purchase the airline tickets as part of a travel package or cruise. You may save some money by doing the entire search, comparisons, and purchase yourself, but you may miss out on certain advantages. Major cruise lines and tour operators contract with airlines to help ensure the availability of seats through primary gateway cities (New York, Atlanta, Miami, Chicago, St. Louis, Dallas/Ft. Worth, Houston, Phoenix, Denver, Los Angeles, San Francisco, Seattle, etc.). The airfares may not be the lowest to be found but the convenience factor does have some value. Cruise lines and tour operators usually offer transfers from the airport to your starting destination (and back the other way when you return). Representatives meet you at the airport and direct you to shuttle buses after you get your luggage. Special arrangements may be made if there has been an unexpected schedule change with the cruise ship or tour operator. However, when you have your own air, you are on your own.

Common Airfare Sources
(in addition to airline information)

www.airfare.com	www.onetravel.com
www.airgorilla.com	www.orbitz.com
www.airlineconsolidator.com	www.priceline.com
www.airlineticketsdirect.com	www.sidestep.com
www.cheapflights.com	www.skyauction.com
www.cheaptickets.com	www.travelbag.co.uk
www.expedia.com	www.travelersnet.com
www.faremax.com	www.travelhub.com
www.flights.com	www.travelocity.com
www.hotwire.com	www.travelzoo.com
www.metafares.com	

Getting the Airline Tickets You Need

Once you have a specific destination in mind, dates of travel, and number of passengers, the search begins. Preliminary information can be obtained by searching the websites of the airlines that are in your area or that you can access. If the information is acceptable that may be all that you need to do. Airlines in the U.S. usually allow you to hold a space for up to 24 hours and that allows you to do additional price comparisons. A typical alternative is to consult Internet search sites such as those listed below. Ideally, you allow from 5 to 6 months prior to your departure to qualify for what may be the best availability and best price. Another alternative is to compare air fares offered by air consolidators who advertise in major newspapers. The alternative suggested above is to take the information gathered to a professional travel consultant who may be able to assist you with a travel package. Since travel consultants are usually not paid a commission by the airlines, you may need to inquire about pricing for the total vacation package. Lower airfares may be possible when combined with hotel, car rental, and other vacation package elements. Frequent flyer miles are not a part of most travel packages and involve a service fee to the travel agent unless you make those arrangements yourself. It is usually recommended that for cruise or tour vacations you schedule arrival one day early so you can be certain of being on time and more rested to begin your vacation. Add a fun city visit to the beginning of your vacation and feel the positive difference. Also, some travel agents say thank you to their clients with travel gifts (flowers, wine, candy, document holders, or ship board credit). That does not happen with you book direct.

On-Time Arrival

Cable News Network (CNN) estimated that 28 to 30 million U.S. passengers traveled by air during the Thanksgiving holiday in 2005. Whatever the occasion, timing is critical if schedules and connections are to be kept within a reasonable tolerance. Airlines do a good job of reliably transporting millions of people daily and every day of the year. Information is available for on-time arrivals and departures at all airports and by airline. Calling first can help you to adjust your schedule and reduce unnecessary airport waiting time. The airline passenger has a challenge to get to the airport with enough time to reliably check in, clear security, and get to the proper departure gate as planned. Making connections can be a challenge as the number of non-stop or direct flights are reduced and financially pressed airlines rely on transportation hubs and computer-projected routes to maximize occupancy.

Back-Ups and Pre-Vacation Basics

Many flights originate very early in the morning and it is the passenger's responsibility to be at the airport well in advance of the reported departure time. The minimum basics for getting to the airport in a timely manner are a good alarm clock, perhaps a hotel wake-up call, maybe a wind-up clock in case of power outage, and possibly a cell phone with an alarm feature. In addition to getting out of the door in a timely fashion, it is essential to avoid traffic delays on the way to the airport. Freeways and expressways can be especially troublesome in case of a jam-up. When timing is critical, consider side streets that may be slower but have more options. Another option is to schedule a one-night Park n' Fly at a participating hotel near the airport. The price of parking is included in the one-night room rate; you get a permit to leave in your car, and the hotel shuttle takes you and your luggage to the airport terminal. You get a restful night at the hotel, a certain wake-up time, breakfast if desired, and a shuttle that is just a short trip to the terminal. But first, double-check your documents. Be certain about the relevant details. Be sure to have the correct passports and/or visas, if needed. The names on the e-tickets or paper tickets must match the government-issued photo-ID. Having the correct travel documents is always the traveler's responsibility.

Get Seat Assignments

Early reservations increase your chances of getting the seating choice you want. For long coach class flights, it may be beneficial to request an aisle seat. Bulkhead and exit row seats may be

requested at the airport check-in desk. A major effort is being made to fill every seat with each flight to generate more income and return the airlines to profitability. To get the reserved seats you want, it is more important than ever to book early and get seat assignments. You might even download the seating map of various aircraft so you will have a visual reference for indicating your preferences as you book. Some seats have more leg room or better visibility of the ground than others. Some seats are on the exit rows and require that you be comfortable with assisting the flight attendants in the case of an emergency and physically able to open a fairly heavy exit door. Bulkhead seats at the front of coach class allow more legroom but may not have reclining seats. Many passengers prefer the aisle seat because of easier access to the restroom and opportunities to get up and stretch legs on those long flights.

Get seat assignments at the time you purchase the ticket whenever possible. It will facilitate electronic check-in and reduce the need to wait in long lines to get a last-minute seat assignment as part of the check-in process. One alternative that seems to be working well is Southwest Airlines' non-seat-assignment plan that is based on having only one class of passenger service and personal choice based on where you position yourself in the boarding line.

Discount Airfare

Best airline rates are something of an illusion now that most airlines are having such protracted financial difficulty due to high cost of doing business and high fuel costs. What used to be four classes of service on each flight is now a much more complex pricing structure that tends to resemble whatever the market will bear. Discount tickets, once purchased, are nonrefundable. One option is to go online after midnight when the "best fares" and new fares may be placed on the market for the first time. Airfares are subject to change hourly as conditions change. It is best to put a reservation hold on a fare that you think is the one you want. Coming back even minutes later may not be sufficient to get the fare you were just quoted.

Super deals such as flights across the country for a very small fare may be legally limited to a few seats only and may be loaded with restrictions. Discount tickets usually include blackout dates, one-way-only tickets that must be purchased for both directions, taxes (included in the tickets), and flight times limited to certain hours or days of the week. Periodic, full-page ads designed mostly to be attention getters create the image that deep discount flights are possible. The underlying intent is to "up-sell" (pressure to spend more or upgrade) your ticket when you do call or go online to make a purchase. Some discount fares, however, may be limited to travel before 7 a.m. and after 5 p.m. and that may not be apparent when you buy a ticket online. The general rule is to be cautious about blackouts and other restrictions that may apply. Read the specific rules for the fare you are purchasing.

Creativity Can Pay Dividends

Some airline routes are clearly more profitable than others. Sometimes you can save money by going to an alternate airport for either departure or arrival. Different airlines will at times provide low-cost fares you can use as they reposition a particular plane. Airlines have a tendency to offer best rates for red-eye flights because of the passenger inconvenience, but mostly so they can reposition that aircraft into a higher traffic airport at times that they can sell more profitable morning tickets. Flights in and out of lower-profile airports can be another way to reduce air fares. Many of the best international fares originate at London airports and you may often find that the most direct route to your destination is not the lowest fare. Some flight segments with large international carriers are also for the purpose of repositioning and may get you the airport that will have the best fare for another segment that you want. Start-up airlines also have great fares as they begin air service. Southwest Airlines, an exceptional discount carrier, has been in business for 38 years.

Frequent Flyer Programs

Dating back to 1981, frequent flyer programs have evolved into one of the most successful advertising and marketing programs of all times. Currently over 80 million consumers consciously seek to earn frequent flyer miles. Originally, the concept was related to fostering airline loyalty and rewarding the frequent "business" flyer to stay with a particular airline. Now, it has become mostly a credit card marketing program to build and hold market share and an incentive to use credit cards for nearly every purchase. For the consumer, the goal has been to get a free airline ticket and, more recently, to upgrade a coach ticket to either business class or first class. Airlines, of course, limit the number of seats available under the program for each flight and have learned that it is basically an advertising cost that is needed to hold market share. This writer's recent attempts to use frequent flyer miles to purchase airline tickets from the West Coast to Europe involved a major bit of frustration. By calling the airline daily the problem was finally resolved and the schedule was secured. It often takes patience to use the frequent flyer miles.

Children Flying Alone

Rules vary for each airline carrier in reference to unaccompanied minors traveling on nonstop, direct, and connecting flights. On nonstop flights no additional fee may be charged. An approved adult may also be authorized to take a child through security and to see that the child is safely aboard. Some airlines are requiring "extra-shepherding service fees." Typically, a fee of approximately $40 to $75 is charged for domestic flights, and a higher fee may be charged for international flights. Alaska Airlines procedures prohibit any minors from flying on the last flight of the day on connecting flights. Special care must be taken well in advance to ensure that all conditions are met and that back-up systems are in place to protect the child's safety. One option is to provide the child with a cell phone and specific, written instructions for one or more persons that will meet the child at his/her final destination. Coordinate with the specific flight attendant who will look after the child's safety. Tipping may also be appropriate at the moment of pairing the child with a specific flight attendant.

Advantage of Paying by Credit Card

Subject to changing rules, if you pay for an airline ticket, cruise, or tour with a credit card and the vendor or supplier takes out bankruptcy, or otherwise fails to perform, you may be eligible for a full refund. However, the refund may be conditional on the purchase being from your home state, or, oddly, within 100 miles of your billing address. Also, current rules require that you must dispute the charge within 60 days of the time that the charge first appears on your statement. When possible, simply request a cancellation of the payment at the first instance that you become aware that a supplier cannot deliver as promised. Persons who pay by check or cash may find that it is impossible to receive more than an absolute token amount of refund, and usually no compensation from a bankruptcy court.

Resolving Disputes

In the unfortunate instance that you feel you need to dispute a charge for a service not delivered, or lost baggage, or major inconvenience including financial or physical injury, immediately write down all of the details. Be sure to document the names, titles, dates, and times of all persons contacted to resolve the dispute issue. Be very realistic in proposing a solution to the disputed issue to the extent that you can, not a free cruise for some inconvenience, such as a carpet stain. Sometimes it's a matter of requesting a different room when you preferred a non-smoker's room, or maybe because there was trouble with the plumbing. Typical "acts of God" don't tend to qualify unless it can be shown that neglect or profound indifference compounded the problem and created an actual loss. Keep in mind that memories well after the fact can be very selective and manager promises that are not in writing are probably not reliable. A verbal agreement to provide a partial refund, a credit, or some other form of compensation is almost impossible to prove well after the fact. Also, if something of value is either lost or possibly "stolen," be fully prepared to document that you had the item and the current value of the item. Most lost luggage is found within 24 hours. Be sure the airline has a way to contact you during that period and beyond.

Does Anyone Read the Fine Print?

Recently, on the CBS program *60 Minutes,* Andy Rooney indicated that if the small print was enlarged to the size of the big print, and the big, bold print headlines were reduced to the size of the small print, few ads would ever receive any attention at all.

ACTUAL EXAMPLE: December, 2005, Northwest Airlines placed a full-page ad in our local paper for "**Sample Fares for Travel on Super Bargain Days**.*" One fare was from Portland [OR] to Omaha for $94.00. Another sample fare was from Portland [OR] to Boston for $159.00. The key feature in that ad, however, is the asterisk, not the price. First, fares are based on "each way" and require a roundtrip purchase. Add $10 per ticket if purchased online. Add $20 per ticket if purchased at the NWA desk. Add $3.20 federal excise tax for each flight segment (i.e., every time the plane lands and takes off). Add security charges of up to $18 per roundtrip, per passenger for Passenger Facility Charges because

Major Airline Websites

Aer Lingus	www.aerlingus.com
Aeroperu	www.aeroperu.com
Air Canada	www.aircanada.com
Air India	www.airindia.com
Air Jamaica	www.airjamaica.com
Air New Zealand	www.airnz.co.nz
Air Pacific	www.airpacific.com
All Nippon	www.fly-ana.com
Aloha	www.alohaairlines.com
Air France	www.airfrance.com
Alitalia	www.alitalia.com
Aeromexico	www.aeromexico.com
Alaska/Horizon	www.alaskaair.com
American	www.amrcorp.com
America West	www.americawest.com
Asiana Airlines	www.asiana.co.ke/english
Austrian	www.aua.com
British Airways	www.britishairways.com
China Airlines	www.china-airlines.com
Continental	www.continental.com
Delta	www.delta.com
Frontier	www.frontierairlines.com
Hawaiian	www.hawaiianair.com
Iberia	www.iberia.com
Japan Airlines	www.jal.com
Jet Blue	www.jetblue.com
KLM Royal Dutch	www.klm.com
Korean Air	www.koreanair.com
Lufthansa	www.lufthansa.com
Malaysia Airlines	www.malaysiaairlines.com
Mexicana	www.mexicana.com
Midway	www.usair/midway
Northwest	www.nwa.com
Quantas	www.quantas.com
SAS	www.sas.com
Singapore	www.singaporeair.com
Southwest	www.southwest.com
Swissair	www.swiss.com
United	www.ual.com
US Airways	www.usairways.com
Virgin Atlantic	www.virginatlantic.com

of the 9/11 terrorist act. The travel window is for a period of less than four weeks.

The main body of the ad says, "A 7-day advance purchase is required and seats are limited…." Next, you ask, "How limited?" It's very possible that as few as two seats per flight are offered. Therefore, you better be quick. Then there was the truly fine print of approximately 600 words that was described as the "Terms and Conditions." The add-on purchase fees are discussed, the fare is limited to the coach class of service, tickets must be paid in full within 24 hours of reservation, blackout dates apply, most fares require a minimum 3-day stay, a Saturday night stay is required on certain dates, stopovers are not permitted, upgrades are not permitted except under certain circumstances, additional taxes and fees apply including an airport improvement fee up to $15, a nonrefundable surcharge will be added for paper tickets in markets where an e-ticket is available, all fees are subject to change without notice, changes can be made for a $100 service fee, tickets are nonrefundable and nontransferable, seats are limited and may not be available, other restrictions may apply, and additional comments are made about the lengthy procedure for applying for a possible best fare that is at least five dollars less on the same day that the ticket was purchased. Traveler's quiz question: *"What is the fare?"* For a great many "discount ads" it is the fine print that is far more important than the large print.

The importance of price can hardly be underestimated. Virtually all consumers have become complacent about constant marketing that suggests the price is discounted, up to 70% off, cheap, incredible savings, and so forth. When it comes to pricing airfares, it seems to make the most sense to think in terms of basic transit or vacation transit. "Cheap airfare" may be suitable for going from Point A to Point B and back. "Vacation airfare" is more about getting the precise schedule that you need, not what the airline offers. It is common for the vacation to begin *after* you get off the airplane and out of the airport. Vacation travel usually involves much more luggage, maybe the whole family, and is focused on leisure and excitement, not just saving a few dollars on the airfare. Keeping the focus on realistic and competitive airfares is one of the ways to help moderate prices in a financially difficult, international market. Spend wisely, vote with your dollars, and enjoy your vacation.

Suggested Additional Resources

www.airfareabroad.com

www.airfarestore.com

www.airgorilla.com

www.airlineconsolidator.com

www.bestfares.com

www.budgettravelonline.com

www.businesstravel.about.com

www.discount-airfare.com

www.economytravel.com

www.frequentflyer.com

www.friendlyplanet.com

www.hotwire.com

www.lowestfare.com

www.priceline.com

www.seatguru.com

www.travelhub.com

www.unclaimedbaggage.com

www.usatoday.com/travel

9
Bike, Hike, Bus, or Motorcoach

I enjoy dirt bike riding, reading classic literature, impressionist art, traveling, and music. —Mandy Moore

The Walking Option

Walking vacations tend to be rare as most North Americans in particular use private cars for nearly everything—including a drive to the store to buy a quart of milk. The overall convenience of the private car, pick-up, SUV, or car and trailer is hard to deny for its ability to transport additional people and bulky things. The ability to carry things on foot tends to limit all accessories to the backpack, tote bag, or a large purse. More physically active touring is one of the best ways to see the world "up close and personal," and is usually restrained only by your imagination.

Adventure Hikes

Hiking, in contrast to pragmatic walking from point to point, enhances scenic imagery, peaceful "escapes," and rigorous physical

exertion for the sheer joy of it. The potential for both national and international hiking tours is limited only by one's imagination. It is the major alternative to so many vehicle-dependent activities that have become the essence of so many travel vacations. One couple, for instance, has recently been in the process of walking across the United States. Their parents are shipping food packages ahead of their journey by one to two days to relieve the burden of carrying heavy supplies needed for daily subsistence. A walker should consume roughly one gallon of water per day when engaged in rigorous physical activity. And since each gallon of water weighs approximately eight pounds, it would soon be a very substantial load just to carry enough liquid for many days of serious hiking.

Endless Hiking Trails

There are a great many books published on hiking trails just about anywhere you would care to go. They are complete with maps, attractions, resources, trail markers, flora and fauna descriptions, and all of the basics for making your hiking experiences a pleasant one. The degree of physical strenuousness and/or skill required will also tend to be spelled out graphically. Samples include the following:

- *Hiking Trails of the Great Smoky Mountains,* by Kenneth Wise
- *North Carolina Hiking Trails, 4th Ed.,* by AMC Hiking Guide Series
- *Guide to the Superior Hiking Trail,* by Andrew Slade
- *Maine Mountain Guide, 9th Ed.,* by Appalachian Mountain Club Books
- *Arizona Hiking: Urban Trails, Easy Paths & Overnight Treks,* by Arizona Highways
- *Hiking Trails II: Southcentral Vancouver Island,* by Richard Blier
- *Utah's Favorite Hiking Trails,* by J. David Day
- *100 Oregon Hiking Trails,* by Don Lowe
- *A Traveler's Guide to the Historic Columbia River Highway,* by Ken Manske

Travel by Bus

Greyhound (800-231-2222 or www.greyhound.com) is the only remaining nationwide bus carrier and they have recently discontinued service to many of the more remote and therefore less profitable routes. Schedules and routes should be checked well in advance and near the time of actual planned travel. Greyhound Bus Lines does not take reservations. To be boarded you must arrive at least one hour before the intended departure and buy a ticket. If needed, an additional bus may be put in service to meet an overload demand. The convenience and economy of inter-city bus trips, however, tends to be lost by the cost of meals and especially lodging to complete a long trip.

Motorcoach Tours

Motorcoach tours, a distinctly different travel medium, may be escorted by a professional tour guide, utilize specific restaurants

and hotels, and follow a well-defined itinerary. A motorcoach is a bus that is specifically designed for touring. Each vehicle usually features large windows, comfortable seating, air conditioning, large luggage compartments, and may have restroom facilities. Some of the more independent motorcoach tours do not have a tour guide escort on the bus, but do meet with guides at each of the scheduled stops. The experience can range from a budget package with budget hotels and restaurants to a luxury travel experience. Motorcoach tours are also one of the best ways to see any foreign destination

Sample Tour Operator Sites

www.azcoachtours.com
www.blueandgoldfleet.com
www.bransonshuttle.com
www.brennanvacations.com
www.busonus.com
www.carsontours.com
www.classiclondontours.com
www.cosmos.com
www.eyre.com
www.globusandcosmos.com
www.globusjournies.com
www.goanderson.com
www.goodtimetours.com
www.grayline.com
www.graylinealaska.com

www.gte.co.uk
www.hlcharter.com
www.hotard.com
www.intercitycoach.co.nz
www.lasvegastourcompany.com
www.looktours.com
www.omca.com
www.phillytour.com
www.qantasvacations.com
www.queenslandertours.com
www.starrtours.com
www.sunshineboston.com
www.tauck.com
www.trafalgar.com
www.trailways.com

"up close and personal" rather than fly over entire areas and perhaps visit a single city.

This Must Be Belgium, If This Is Tuesday

There has long been the stereotyped image of trying to see and do too much by motorcoach in Europe and of losing track of what country you happen to be visiting. Tour companies continue to revise their itineraries to accommodate travelers who want to spend several days in each of a few cities instead of changing hotels every night. Most motorcoach tours, however, offer exciting itineraries, schedules that range from flexible to highly structured, appealing restaurants and hotels along the way, and professional tour guides to keep the experience entertaining, informative, and far more personalized than you could get from books and brochures. Travel in deluxe motorcoaches is one of the best ways to become familiar with a new area, its people, and distinctive features. You don't have to watch every road sign to stay on track and avoid becoming lost. You don't have to randomly select restaurants, hotels, special places of interest, or find a place to park. A great many friendships have also been formed almost by chance as a specific group of people is engaged in leisure activities and new experiences that suddenly gives you much in common with your fellow travelers. The depth of the leisure travel satisfaction that is possible is evident from the high percentage of motorcoach travelers who repeat the experience.

Different Styles of Motorcoach Tours

Choosing the right type of motorcoach tour is one of the most important considerations. Additional options include price, itineraries, season, and preferred activities (e.g., scenic tour, sports fan, gambling, entertainment, or special interest).

• **The Independent Tour** is for the traveler who is comfortable with making his/her own arrangements, likes the freedom to make changes, and is familiar with the destination and its attractions. Popular destinations for independent tours include Las Vegas, Palm Springs, Mexican resorts, and Hawaii. The degree of independence will vary among tour companies and different destinations and variables such as a combination tour of rail, rental car, and hotel with your own start and end dates.

• **The Hosted Tour** is perhaps best suited for the traveler who wants to plan ahead yet have many details pre-arranged such as hotels and hotel staff or tour guides who can suggest optional activities. The traveler is able to make some adjustments to his/her own departure date, length of stay, and specifics about level of accommodations.

• **The Escorted Tour** is likely to appeal most to the traveler who wants to have the entire vacation experience planned in advance, is comfortable traveling with the same group, and enjoys getting better acquainted with a distinct group of fellow travelers. A tour guide will escort the entire trip.

Bicycle Travel Groups

Organized bicycle rides are another growing trend for adults who want a change of pace, up close and personal contact with their immediate surroundings, and the camaraderie of like

---

Samples Bicycle Tour Websites

www.adv-cycling.org/tours
www.bicyclinglife.com
www.bikechina.com
www.bikemaps.com
www.bikemaui.com
www.bikenewyork.com
www.biketour-reviews.com
www.discoverfrance.com

www.easyridertours.com
www.irondonkey.com
www.ohiobike.org
www.topbicycle.com
www.travelersdigest.com
www.triumphbiketours.com
www.winecountrybikes.com

---

participants who find safety and friendships in an organized group activity. One typical method of planning a travel route is to pre-arrange motel or hotel space for the bicyclists at reasonable intervals of maybe 50 to 75 miles per day to allow the participants a certain place to sleep for the night, to wash up and tend to any and all personal needs before starting out on the next day's adventure. Pre-set destinations for each day allow the fastest and the slowest riders to not interfere with each other. On these tours the rider's luggage is transported by motor vehicle to a pre-determined stopping place for the end of each day's ride.

Unique Hotel Properties

Casual and not-so-casual roadside stops can include bed-and-breakfast properties, boutique hotels, clean and safe three-star hotels, and campsites. These smaller, typically non-franchised properties can be great for local lore, family-style dining, uniqueness, and generally offer a choice of locations that can tie in with the outdoorsy activity you may have in mind. Small hotels and motels located in small towns along your route are often near the hub of activities for that particular community and may place you within easy walking distance to interesting restaurants and cafes and mom-and-pop retailers of all sorts that are tending to vanish from large urban areas.

Boutique hotels are smaller, tourist-oriented properties with a distinctive look, feel, and perhaps a lot of local history. Generally, these are not to be confused with budget properties since the cost of completely renovating historic buildings is very high and staying there gives a distinct flavor for your entire vacation. As in much travel anywhere in the world, it is the interesting people you meet along the way that give you special memories, sometimes lasting friends, and a whole new dimension to your life experiences. Often, you will find yourself exchanging e-mails or other correspondence for years to come as you quickly acquire a shared experience with fellow travelers.

Camping Under the Stars
Campsites are much improved from the little clearing where our pioneer ancestors might pitch a tent and build a campfire for the night. Today, the major service provided by organized campsites is the provision of full utilities. This includes public toilets, showers,

laundromats, scenic play areas, maybe a kitchen, and all in a park-like setting with legal parking that is off the highway. Some properties will have a swimming pool, hot tub, place to exercise or watch television, or do your own barbeque. Typically there are spaces set aside for the children to play and the pets to run, or just a place to relax and sleep comfortably off the road. The website www.freecampgrounds.com lists 937 campsites across the

U.S. KOA has hundreds of campgrounds across the U.S. and international locations as well (see: www.koacampgrounds.com). The U.S. Army Corps of Engineers maintains roughly 53,000 campsites near lakes, rivers, and oceans. Good Sam Parks are another option.

Travel by Foot, Taxi, and Public Transportation

Lots of options exist around the world to travel by trolley, subway, monorail, city tour bus, and public buses without needing to rent a car, or navigate in strange territory with different laws and then randomly search for places to park, to eat, or to rest whenever you want. Public conveyances and some private tour vehicles often let you get on and off as desired so you can explore further on foot and still have a way back to your original departure point. The subway  system in Vienna, for instance, was started about 1895 and continues to be a great service that is readily used by locals and tourists. In Mexico the public bus system is very reasonably priced and was recently at 4 pesos compared to a 50-peso taxi ride. Another option for the traveler with a penchant for walking is to contract with a taxi driver for a fixed price to take you around to places that you want to see (avoid relying too heavily on the taxi driver as they would mostly take you to their favorite vendors and flea markets). Pay the driver when the trip is complete, not in advance. Or, in Juneau, Alaska, you can travel up an 1,800-foot hillside in a gondola within minutes and for a very modest ticket price. The ticket is also good all day so you can go back in the evening and see the city lights as well. In both Malacca, Malaysia, and Beijing, China, this writer has ridden in bicycle-drawn rickshaws that are ideal for moving at a slow pace and on streets that would be too narrow for a car. In more esoteric places such as Mongolia you might contract to ride a camel.

Serious Walking Attire

A basic rule worth noting is that a walking-oriented journey should start with good quality shoes (or boots) that are comfortably broken-in and designed for the type of walking or climbing activity that you are most likely to do. One good slip in the wrong place that is caused by poorly designed shoes is enough to spoil an otherwise great vacation. Function is always more important than style for being a physically active traveler. Spike heels may be wonderful at a wedding or very formal dinner, but are especially treacherous on cobblestone, or rocky, graveled trails. Flip-flops may be functional at the beach or next to the pool and locker room, but are likewise prone to contributing to accidents on rough surfaces. Good quality sandals can be safe in many brief walking situations and provide great ventilation for the feet, but can be a real nuisance when little bits of gravel get between the bottom of a foot and the insole of the sandal. The absence of a heel can also make sandals a bit more slippery than regular shoes, especially if the soles are made of leather.

Dress for Comfort

Comfortable clothing is much the same in nearly all parts of the world. Consider the fact that clothing, especially casual clothing, is manufactured all over the world and looks much the same everywhere. Very loose clothing may have appeal for some situations but is prone to catching on something unexpectedly and might lead to a severe injury. There are minimum standards of community sensibilities in some parts of the world that are distinctly different from ours. In Islamic

countries, for instance, it is flagrant disregard of their religion for tourists to travel in shorts, especially short shorts. Sleeveless shirts or blouses, or any clothing that exposes certain parts of the body, may likewise be offensive. In most of the world's churches, mosques, synagogues, and other places of worship, it may not be appropriate for men to wear hats indoors and may be required for women to wear some form of head covering. In travel to unfamiliar parts of the world, be attentive to local customs for appropriate style of dress. Careful observation of your surroundings will almost certainly suggest what is likely to be appropriate. At a restaurant in Kuala Lumpur, a gentleman in our group was provided with a loaner pair of long pants before being seated. In that restaurant, within an Islamic region of the world, it was not acceptable for a man to wear travel shorts to a luncheon meal.

Additional Suggested References

www.activenewzealand.com
www.affordabletours.com
www.alaskasummer.com
www.auswalk.com
www.backpackertours.com
www.brindisi.ca
www.ciclismoclassico.com
www.coachusa.com
www.grandcanyontourcompany.com
www.greentortoise.com
www.greyhound.com

www.hawaiianwalkways.com
www.historictours.com/boston/
www.irishtourism.com
www.oldtowntrolley.com
www.starlinetours.com
www.timberwolftours.com
www.trafalgar.com
www.trolleytours.com
www.waikikitrolley.com
www.walkingconnection.com

10
Train Travel

I love to travel, but hate to arrive. — Albert Einstein

The Romance of Travel by Rail

In the U.S. from roughly 1850 to 1950 travel by rail was typically the fastest, smoothest, and most cost-effective means of transportation available for long and short distances. There is a certain nostalgia for the Doppler Effect of the train's whistle. There was the powerful image of the streamlined diesel locomotive cruising through America's diverse landscape. Eventually, there was the Vista Dome car that gave passengers a panoramic view of the changing scene and the chance to walk about comfortably, drink, dine, and even sleep aboard Pullman coaches, if desired. The interstate highway system and evolution of jet aircraft transportation that was seriously underway in the 1950s altered the passenger profitability factor for the railroads.

The Struggle to Compete

Amtrak was reorganized on May 1, 1971, with major government subsidies that have been insufficient for this rail passenger

service to show a profit. Obviously, there are areas of the U.S. with greater potential for profit, but it was not in the national interest to operate only in select areas of the country. Like the financial dilemma with the airlines, the population of the U.S. is not evenly distributed and capital expenditures and operating costs for railroads are extremely high. The cost of crossing mountain ranges and vast expanses of farmland or desert, where populations are sparse, greatly adds to the cost of serving major population centers. Serving the East and West Coast and populated areas of the Midwest have the greatest potential for profitable passenger train service, but connecting all of the major population centers puts the overall operating cost in the red. For additional details, see their website at www.amtrak.com and then call your travel agent.

Basic Amtrak Facts
- Amtrak (1-800-872-7245) serves over 500 stations in 46 states (exceptions are Hawaii, South Dakota, Wyoming, and Alaska).
- Daily passenger ridership averages 68,000. Total passengers for 2005 were almost 26 million.
- Amtrak operates over 22,000 miles of track, but owns less than 3% of that track.
- Amtrak operates 24/7 and every day of the year.

Cost vs. Time
Other major factors are time, speed and a multiplicity of stops. The Amtrak from Los Angeles to Portland, Oregon, a trip of approximately 1,200 miles, takes about 27.5 hours, or an average of more than 43 miles per hour. Still, that can be a very long time to be in and out of one passenger seat and probably requires about three meals. The cost is increased very substantially if a sleeper coach is involved. From Chicago to Miami, Florida, the estimated travel time for Amtrak going by way of Washington, D.C., is 44.3 hours. By booking sleeping accommodations, you become a first-class passenger and can have a very pleasant trip.

Reported Amtrak Highlights Since 2002
- A reduction of personnel by almost 5,000.
- The development of a detailed and prioritized five-year capital plan focused on restoring the NE Corridor to necessary levels

of reliability and safety, and on restoration of an aging fleet of rolling stock used throughout the system.
- Termination of the mail and express operation (not profitable).
- Elimination or truncation of three long-distance routes.
- Increased ridership from 22.5 million in 2000 to 25.1 million in 2004.
- Federal financial support has increased from $831 million in FY02 to $1.2 billion in FY05.

Source: David Gunn's memorandum to the Amtrak Board of Trustees

American Orient Express

The American Orient Express, a private luxury train, has progressed through several resurrections and has been finding great success in the travel industry. Chief Executive Officer Henry Hillman, Jr. acquired the line in 1997 and has since expanded service in 2005 to 10 itineraries and four theme tours. Most but not all overnights are onboard the train (actually a red train and a blue train). Sample itineraries and theme tours are as follows:

- Antebellum South
- Autumn in New England and Quebec
- Best of the Canadian Rockies
- Civil War and the South
- Coastal Culinary Explorer
- Copper Canyon and Colonial Mexico
- Grand Trans-Canada Rail Journey
- Jazz Heritage and Southern Culture
- Murder on the American Orient Express
- National Parks of the West
- Pacific Coast Explorer
- The Great Northwest and Rockies
- The Great Transcontinental Rail Journey

American Orient Express is North America's only private luxury train, except for a few very short rail line trains operating on a strictly regional basis. AOE tours typically range from $100 to $350 per person per day plus airfare. The restored vintage railcars are from an earlier era and include deluxe sleeping accommodations, elegant dining car with onboard chefs, a lounge car with fully stocked bar, a glass-enclosed dome car, and observation car.

The Lingering Mystique of Rail Travel

The famous Orient Express, made even more famous by Agatha Christie's *Murder on the Orient Express,* has long been noted for being the ultimate in rail travel. This unique European rail line originated in 1883, and eventually traveled roundtrip from Paris to Istanbul. Many times it was threatened financially because of luxury-level cost and competition with airlines. As recently as June, 2001, the Orient Express was limited to the Paris to Vienna route. There was a great risk that the famed Orient Express would fade into history. Fortunately for history buffs and rail travel buffs alike,

the world-famous Orient Express is still listed in the 2006 European railway timetables. Also, there is a competing rail line called Venice Simplon Orient Express (VSOE, Ltd.) that travels from London to Venice. If you are considering either rail line, it is recommended that you research both lines carefully to be sure you get what you want.

EuroRail is noted for running on schedule and for being a very efficient mode of travel in Europe. The flexible ticket or Europass (now called Eurail Selectpass) allows you to choose from five bordering countries in Western and Eastern Europe out of a total of 22 countries.

92

Additional information can be found at www.raileurope.com. Saver and Youth passes are also available.

Additional options include Via Rail Canadian Rail Tours; Japan's Bullet Train (Acela) with speeds up to 345 mph; Spanish Talgo (218 mph); Eurostar (188 mph); Australia's Speedrail TGV (225 mph), or the Trans-Siberian which takes about 5.5 days to go

from Moscow to Vladivostok. There is also the Alaska White Pass Railroad (tour train) which was once a narrow-gauge mining train. The Alaska Railroad has two rail cars that are owned by Princess Cruise Line that takes passengers from the ship to one of their scenic lodges in Denali State Park. Holland America and Royal Caribbean also have rail cars on the Alaska Railroad train and they provide similar tour packages. Smaller, scenic rail opportunities exist in many parts of the world and even on the small island of St. Kitts in the Caribbean.

Additional Sources of Information

www.alaskarailroad.com
www.americanorientexpress.com
www.bluetrain.co.za
www.coppercanyontours.com
www.gsmr.com
www.luxury-train-travel.co.uk
www.maineeasternrailroad.com
www.mircorp.com

www.princesslodges.com
www.privaterailcars.net
www.railexcursions.com
www.rockymountaineer.com
www.romaniantrip.com
www.traintraveling.com/australia
www.trainweb.com
www.vacationsbyrail.com

11
Cruise Ships

I am one of those who never knows the direction of my journey until I have almost arrived. —Anna Louise Strong

Tour all seven continents and over 1,500 ports of call. Why settle for a vacation in one spot when you can relax on a cruise, enjoy great food, entertainment, and see multiple destinations?

The Dream Vacation

Cruising has become a model for the dream vacation. The increasing popularity of cruising is proportionate to the benefits received. Camaraderie among fellow passengers on a voyage of discovery is just one factor. There is the unmatched relaxation of the all-inclusive cruising experience. Just unpack once to see multiple ports of call. For one affordable price, the cruise passenger chooses from a whole host of exciting activities, gourmet foods, and classy entertainment. There is the pampering and service that relates to individual tastes and people of all ages and backgrounds. A cruise is a floating resort with exciting sights, sounds, and a sense of adventure that is uniquely different from the day-to-day world at home. The ship becomes the stress-free vehicle that allows you to explore new parts of the world. If the perceived high cost of cruising is keeping you away from the actual details, compare with the cost of one Super Bowl (2006) ticket. There were 65,000 tickets sold for Super Bowl XL in Detroit, Michigan. The non-season-holder price for a 50-yard line seat *started* at $3,500. Consider the suggestions in this book and you can make a cruise the vacation the one that is remembered long after you return.

The "Love Boat" Image of Cruising

Many of you may recall the original "Love Boat" series that aired on television from 1977-86 for a total of 249 episodes. It starred Gavin MacLeod as Capt. Merrill Stubing and a diverse cast of actors including Fred Grandy as "Gopher." The actual ship scenes were filmed aboard the Pacific Princess, a ship that was retired from the Princess fleet in the Fall of 2002 after 27 years of service. There was also a second generation entitled "The Love Boat: The Next Wave." That short-lived version aired on television from 1998-99 for a total of 25 episodes. John Urich starred as Capt. Jim Kennedy III.

In the real world, more than 3,000 brides and grooms have been married aboard Princess Cruises since 1998. The numbers for cruising in general continue to grow at a dramatic rate. Cruise Lines International Association (CLIA) projects 12 million cruise passengers for the year 2006.

Consider These Cruising Numbers

The "big picture" for cruising is very impressive. Cruise Lines International Association reports annual cruise passenger growth as follows:

2002	7,640,000
2003	8,195,000
2004	9,107,000

CLIA also reports that the average cruise passenger growth rate from 1980-2004 has been +8.2%. The potential for growth is huge because a big majority of Americans have not yet taken their first cruise. The number of cruise ship passengers from the U.S. continues to rise each year, and there is still 88% of the American population that has not gone on a cruise. Another positive indicator is that cruise lines continue to expand their fleets and passenger capacity each year. It is a safe prediction that you, as the reader of this book, *will* be among the growing minority who will cruise in the near future.

Why You Might Want to Cruise (or Cruise Again)

- Opportunities to see exciting destinations that are often accessible only by cruise ship.
- The appeal of fabulous cuisine and a chance to relax in romantic, adventuresome settings.
- Broadway/Las Vegas style entertainment, music, dancing, comedians, and specialty acts.
- Scenic views, new experiences, chance to meet new and interesting people having fun.
- Opportunities for sunbathing, active sports, or just relaxation in a carefree setting.
- Personal service, housekeeping, and generally being pampered especially at mealtime.
- Unpack only once and be free of job responsibilities and household tasks.
- Allowing someone else to provide the transportation and attend to all of the travel details.
- Opportunity to share a wide range of activities with others who are enjoying themselves.
- Discovering new people and places and recording photographic images of your adventures.
- Visit the spa, exercise room, and pools. Enjoy the moment in a deck chair with a book.
- Consider games of chance in the casino, play bingo, participate in the ship's activities.

- Experience new ports of call, sun-filled beaches, snorkeling, glaciers, and sea kayaking.
- Shop as often or as infrequently as you like in great settings for taking photographs.
- Go for family fun, value, safety, great food, and entertainment in a stress-free package.

The Practical Side of Cruising

Cruising, when matched with *comparable* land-based vacations, typically *COSTS LESS*. The way to verify for yourself is to total all land-based vacation costs (airfare, hotel, all meals, all transportation, all entertainment, all tips, all incidentals, and all admission prices or park passes). When you get a total figure, divide by the number of days. Next, do the same thing with your cruise cost. Not only is the cruising figure potentially lower, but the quality of food tends to be better, entertainment is more varied, children enjoy the total experience more, and the cruise vacation is far more relaxing.

Cruising is comparable to being an honored guest aboard a floating resort hotel—and much more. It is the ultimate all-inclusive vacation for couples, groups, children, and for those traveling solo. According to Cruise Lines International Association (CLIA) over one million children cruised in 2002. By 2004, CLIA projected that 1.1 million children age 17 and younger have sailed on major cruise ships. Children often become so engrossed with the interesting and well-supervised programs designed specifically for them that they seem to "disappear" into their own world of cruising. For adults, the "romantic side of cruising" is in having so many great choices of activities for everyone, regardless of age.

You board a cruise ship with a plastic key card (your computerized ID card, digitized door key, and ship's credit card rolled into one card). Friendly cruise-staff members will greet you, provide information, and encourage you to explore the ship. Your luggage will be delivered to your stateroom or suite. The ship will soon get underway and you will move effortlessly from one exciting port to another in complete comfort. When your luggage arrives at your stateroom, you unpack and stow your suitcases under the bed. As you explore the vast amenities and diversities of your ship, there are choices to be made. Where to eat? What to do? When to do it? Go to a music lounge? Just sit and watch people, or go to the Excursion Desk for additional information about day trips in your ports of call. Perhaps you can schedule a spa appointment, sunbathe on the deck, explore the ship's public areas, and choose among all of the options for food, drink, and enjoying the great views.

Each evening you will receive a pamphlet describing all of the next day's events. There are continuous offerings of activities, entertainment, and options for great dining at traditional or open seating restaurants, buffets, and more. Activities will vary somewhat with each ship and the particular itinerary. Activities include spas, pools, sunbathing, sports, children's programs, live music, classes, movie theater, cable television, shopping, library book and movie selections, card or board games, shuffleboard, and wine tasting. Believe it or not, all of Royal Caribbean's Voyager class of ships have a permanent ice-skating rink, ice shows, and a rock climbing wall.

Once underway, there is the informal casting-off party as many of the passengers go to upper decks to view the harbor as it begins to fade into the background. The outdoor musical entertainment starts, passengers mingle, and the fun and sense of new possibilities begins. Also, as the ship is underway, the onboard shopping mall opens, the casinos open, the buffets continue in full swing, and most people begin to settle into a relaxed and upbeat experience that might be described as a "positive state of mind."

Gourmet-quality evening meals are followed by Broadway/ Vegas style entertainment, and a good night's sleep at sea. There are options for day trips (shore excursions) for most of the ports of call. You can also plan your own walking or taxi tour, or purchase an excursion from a local vendor once you are ashore. The overall cruising experience is one that you will typically treasure and remember for a long time. The diversity of options are so great that each person comes away with his/her own unique experience, memories, and new friendships.

Cruising Success Story

In the business history of the world there are few stories that compare to the success of Carnival Cruise Line. In 1972 Carnival Cruise Lines began its maiden voyage out of the Port of Miami with their only ship—TSS Mardi Gras—and ran aground on a sandbar just outside of the city. From that inauspicious beginning, Carnival, The Fun Ships, have moved on to become the World's Leading Cruise Line. In addition to alliances and/or ownership interests in six other cruise lines (Costa, Cunard, Holland America, Princess Cruises, The Yachts of Seabourn, and Windstar Cruises), Carnival operates the following cruise ships under the Carnival name: Celebration, Conquest, Destiny, Elation, Ecstasy, Fantasy, Fascination, Glory, Holiday, Imagination, Inspiration, Legend, Jubilee, Miracle, Paradise, Pride, Sensation, Spirit, Triumph, Victory, and Valor. Projected for early 2007 is Carnival's Freedom.

Carnival's nearest competitor, the combined fleets of Royal Caribbean International (RCI) and Celebrity Cruise Line, have 20 and 9 ships respectively. RCI has Adventure of the Seas, Enchantment of the Seas (recently stretched 73 feet), Explorer of the Seas, Freedom of the Seas (2006), Grandeur of the Seas, Legend of the Seas, Majesty of the Seas, Mariner of the Seas, Monarch of the Seas, Navigator of the Seas, Radiance of the Seas, Rhapsody of the Seas, Serenade of the Seas, Sovereign of the Seas, Splendour of the Seas, Vision of the Seas, and Voyager of the Seas. Celebrity Cruise Lines has the Century, Constellation, Galaxy, Horizon, Infinity, Mercury, Millennium, Summit, and Zenith. In the third annual Reader's Choice Award by *Travel Weekly* (January 16, 2006), Royal Caribbean International was the top vote-getter for the third consecutive year in the categories of overall, domestic, and Caribbean. Celebrity's Constellation was voted the number one cruise ship overall in the same poll. The above list of cruise ships is subject to change and should be verified to confirm current ownership or other details that may be of interest to the reader.

Major Blue Water (salt water) and River Cruise Lines

The following is a summary of the major cruise lines that are typically available to North American passengers: Princess, Norwegian, Royal Caribbean, Oceania, Regent Seven Seas, Carnival, Holland America, Celebrity, Viking River, Cunard, Amadeus, Costa, Avalon, Star Clipper, Orion, Crystal, Disney, Orient Lines, American Cruise, Uniworld, Windjammer, Yachts of Seabourn, Silversea, Cruise West, American West Steamboat, WindStar, MSC Italian, Peter Deilmann, RiverBarge, Norwegian Coastal Voyage, Delta Queen, and many smaller companies worth considering. See website listings at the end of this chapter for additional details. This list is subject to change. Check with your travel consultant or directly with the cruise ship websites for the most current information.

Direct Cruise Booking Can Cost You Money

A cruise consultant at your local travel agency (who charges little or no fee) may be able to offer fares that are not available to individuals who call the cruise line directly. There is also the likelihood of missing out on shipboard credits, departure gifts, and perhaps a complimentary shore tour that a cruise agency may offer. Another distinction is that experienced cruise consultants provide personal attention for individualized needs that is rarely found at a cruise line call center or website. Personal attention can include matching your preferences with the right cruise line, ship, suite or stateroom selection, and the right dining choices. Assistance can also be provided with flight arrangements, pre- and post-cruise stays, greater selections of shore excursions, and reliable answers to your questions. If still in doubt, make a thorough comparison with all of the details, and then decide.

An agency that specializes in cruise travel will assist you with the entire booking and travel experience. The professional travel consultant can compare multiple cruise lines, multiple itineraries, and competing amenities that may be a best fit and a better price.

The big, flashy, discount price for a budget cruise does not disclose the total cost. Full week cruises that are offered at $499, $599, and $699 per person are based on the expectation of generating additional onboard revenue from the bar, casino, retail purchases, excursions, art auctions, and even soda drinks. Discretionary costs are just that—use your own judgment. Cruise passengers often find that total costs are somewhat above the lowest anticipated cost, but not out of control. A couple celebrating a special anniversary is not likely to be content with an inside stateroom, bunk beds, no window, no balcony, and no shore trips. Cruising is actually a different experience for each person, and there are many personalized choices to be made.

Passport Required by Cruise Passengers to Enter U.S.

New rules for foreign travel by U.S. citizens could affect you now. The U.S. government rules regarding the need for passports to exit and re-enter the U.S. are currently being revised. For the most up-to-date information, U.S. citizens may visit www.travel.state.gov/passport/passport, or call the National Passport Information Center at 1-877-487-2778, or TDD/TYY: 1-888-874-7793. Foreign nationals can contact their government consulate offices for specific details.

Reasons to Get Your Passport Now
- Avoid missing a last-minute travel opportunity, or rush fees to accelerate the application.
- New rules are inevitable and should be checked well in advance of setting travel dates.
- A passport could facilitate a vacation trip to Canada, Mexico, or a cruise.
- Passport fees are now $97 but are valid for ten years. A fee of $67 is needed for renewal.
- It is your best government-issued ID for the changing security screening guidelines of TSA.
- Passports are often required to exit the U.S., or to legally enter most foreign countries.

- Allow 60-90 days after you complete all requirements, provide photos, and pay fees.
- Obtain an "Application for a US Passport" at the post office, online, or other facility.

Cruising Styles

Each cruise line has a distinctive personality or feel about it that is most evident as you vacation from one cruise line to another. Norwegian Cruise Lines (NCL), for instance, has made distinct efforts to encourage freestyle cruising. Each NCL ship has emphasized the possibilities for dining at many different restaurants onboard and at a time you choose. There is more flexibility with respect to time of dining, seating arrangements, and informality of dress (cruise casual). The feeling is similar to that found in many land-based restaurants, and there is a cover charge at some of these onboard restaurants. Carnival Cruise Line has tended to lead the way in flexibility of scheduling and casual informality. RCI and Celebrity rely more on traditional seating that encourages building of friendships with the same group of people each night for dinner and have a tendency to encourage more formality than NCL or Carnival. Celebrity will likewise tend to schedule more optional formal nights for portraits and evening meals than RCI. To really emphasize traditional cruising and even more emphasis on formality, consider Cunard Line (Queen Elizabeth II and Queen Mary II).

Cruising is not a stuffy experience. High ratios of onboard staff work diligently and for long hours to assist all passengers in having a great vacation experience. The "dress code" is casual (sometimes called cruise casual or resort casual) most of the time and allows for swimsuits, flip-flops, souvenir or logo T-shirts, shorts, blue jeans, and even a tropical print shirt. The exception is the dining room, where shorts, tank tops, swimsuits, and blue jeans may be discouraged or restricted, especially at the evening meal. The brochure images of men in tuxedos or dark suits and women in formal dress clothing is a cruising tradition to encourage formal portraits, and the distinctiveness of one or more formal evening meals. Formality has diminished on many of the cruise lines as specialty restaurants become more of an alternative to traditional dining. A major focus of the cruise lines is on enhancing the vacation experience in ways that are distinctive to cruising, yet tailored to what passengers want. If the total experience feels right for you, then it is right. The expansion of home port cruising continues to make this stylish form of vacation even more attractive when airfares can be reduced or even eliminated. What is your next vacation plan going to be?

Additional Suggested Resources

www.americancruiselines.com
www.americanweststeamboat.com
www.avalonwaterways.com
www.bluelagooncruises.com
www.carnival.com
www.celebritycruises.com
www.clippercruise.com
www.coastalvoyage.com
www.costacruises.com
www.cruisecritic.com
www.cruisereviews.com
www.cruisewest.com
www.crystalcruises.com
www.cunard.com
www.deilmann-cruises.com
www.deltaqueen.com
www.disneycruise.com
www.galasea.com
www.hollandamerica.com
www.msccruises.com
www.ncl.com (Norwegian)

www.oceaniacruises.com
www.orientlines.com
www.orioncruises.com
www.portreviews.com
www.princess.com
www.riverbarge.com
www.royalcaribbean.com
www.rssc.com
www.seabourn.com
www.seadreamyachtclub.com
www.silversea.com
www.smallshipcruises.com/
    amadeus
www.starclippers.com
www.starcruises.com
www.uniworld.com
www.victoriacruises.com
www.vikingrivercruises.com
www.windjammer.com
www.windstarcruises.com

12
Hotels and Resorts

*But why, oh why, do the wrong people travel, when the right
people stay at home?* —Noel Coward, *Sail Away*

Not All Stars Shine As Bright

Hotels are often rated by a 3-, 4-, or 5-star system to provide a quick, shorthand method of comparing properties from one city to another. The ratings are not very consistent from one property to

another, or from one area to another. The hotels often rate themselves and may do so more on price than a composite of all amenities and services available. Less than 3-star may simply refer to a budget property with few amenities and little more than a small room with basic bed and bathroom facilities. Independent motel/hotel properties will have greater variability and can range from the clean, safe, and functional to rundown, marginal areas and a potentially uncomfortable place to spend the night. Low rates, especially well below "rack rates," are often found among such properties but may spoil a leisure vacation. Three stars in some

parts of the world are not the same as in the U.S. Anything less than a 4 star plus property in a "third-world country" may not be the experience that you were anticipating. For reviews of hotels, resorts, and bed-and-breakfasts, consider a search on www.tripadvisor.com.

Get What You Want and Need

It's a very big help to know your personal safety and comfort levels in advance. Often, it will be worth a bit more to be well located and spend much less on ground transportation, or worrying about the neighborhood.

Smaller, well-located hotels with one or more restaurants may likewise save transit time and money. A continental breakfast, for instance, is often all that is needed to get a day started. Smaller and mid-size properties without a strong, high-profile edge in the marketplace may be more receptive to an extra night for free or offer reduced rates. One of the primary tricks is to assertively negotiate for discounts as a senior, AAA, or AARP discount, reward nights, Entertainment Card, or any possible promotion that may be in effect. Watch for seasonal discounts that don't conflict with major holidays, conventions, special events, or some sudden surge of business travel. Consider hotels that may be equipped to allow higher density without raising the rate. When traveling in Europe the rooms tend to be smaller, or much smaller than in the U.S., and it may be more difficult to accommodate children. Also, in Europe a quad room is usually too small for four people to occupy. It works out better to rent a suite with an extra room. If unbiased review information is not available, one of the safest strategies is to book with the extremely large hotel/motel chains.

The Caught-in-the-Middle Properties

Mid-range motel and hotel properties that must compete with each other under Internet booking systems are likely to be comfortable, reliable, and to contribute to the feeling that you are having a successful vacation. Mid-range properties are much more inclined to renovate and upgrade mattresses, bedding, towels, carpet, and all furnishings intended to provide a comfortable stay. Additional amenities may include well-operating elevators, swimming pool, hot tub, wireless Internet connections, a view, airport shuttle, and the rudiments of basic concierge services. Hotel satisfaction rests heavily on matching lifestyles and being comparable to vacation properties that you have rented in the past. Apply your personal preferences and the basic rules for getting a good room rate.

Do your best to economize based on supply and demand, season of the year, and time of day (or night). Consumer discounts also apply to mid-range properties. Each hotel room can have up to 40 different prices other than the highest-scheduled rack rate. Find the negotiating technique that works best for you.

Checklist of Variable Hotel Features to Consider

- Access to airport
- Access to major attractions
- Accessibility features
- Additional costs
- Arrangements for children and/ or pets
- Balcony or veranda
- Bed sizes, number, and type
- Bedding type, pillows
- Butler service
- Cocktail lounge
- Concierge service
- Continental breakfast
- Date built or last renovations
- Ease of reservation
- Entertainment on site
- Full bar on site
- High tea
- History of the property
- Indoor or outdoor pool
- Internet access
- Jacuzzi-style bath
- Laundry services
- Location
- Locking room safe
- Luxury, mid-range, or budget
- Meeting or conference rooms
- Neighborhood features and resources
- Parking, shuttle, and taxi services
- Promotions or special rates
- Proximity to shopping.
- Restaurants on site
- Room service
- Security features on site
- Smoking vs. non-smoking
- Spa services
- Spaciousness of rooms
- Television, DVD
- View

There are many hotels that can be readily identified by Internet search of the city or cities that you will be visiting, directories of international hotels, and your professional travel consultant. Invest some time in reading the online reviews of specific properties that interest you. Learning what someone else just paid to stay at a particular property is one of the best negotiating tools to have in your repertoire.

Luxury Properties

The distinguishing factor for most luxury properties is not price alone. Important features include service, amenities, and location. Successful luxury hotel providers routinely offer excellence in service, expected amenities, concierge service, doorman, valet parking, possible butler services, fine dining, a fully stocked cocktail

Hotels That May Exceed Your Expectations
Well-known properties in the U.S. with a particular
reputation to maintain include the following:

Best Western
Choice Hotels International
Coast Hotels and Resorts
Conrad
Courtyard
Crowne Plaza Hotels & Resorts
Delta Hotels
Doubletree
Embassy Suites
Fairfield Inn
Fairmont Hotels & Resorts
Fiesta Americana
Fiesta Inn
Four Points Hotels by Sheraton
Hampton Inn
Hampton Inn & Suites
Hilton
Hilton Garden Inn
Hilton Grand Vacation Club
Holiday Inn Express Hotels
Holiday Inn Hotels
Homewood Suites by Hilton

Hyatt Hotels & Resorts
InterContinental Hotels and Resorts
Kimpton Group Hotels
Marriott Hotels Resorts and Suites
Marriott Vacation Club
Preferred Hotels & Resorts World-
 wide
Princess Alaska Lodges
Red Lion Hotels & Inns
Renaissance Hotels
Residence Inn
Scandic
Sheraton
Sheraton Hotels & Resorts
Shilo Inns & Resorts
Silver Legacy
Springhill Suites
St. Regis/Luxury Collection
Staybridge Suites by Holiday Inn
Towne Place Suites
West Coast Hotels
Wyndham Hotels & Resorts

lounge, live entertainment, exclusivity, and special attention to
décor, large rooms, and all features being offered. Pricing is in the
high to very high range yet is less of a factor for guest satisfaction
than service, service, and more service. The total number of such
properties would be difficult to calculate, but prime examples of
such world-famous hotels would include those listed below.

Inquire about the features and amenities that are important to
you and minimize the chance of being billed for services that you
don't want and don't use. When in doubt, read Internet and travel
magazine reviews of specific properties that you may be considering
before you book. Be sure the property is child friendly, or pet

Hotel Corporate Size May Be an Indicator of Reliability

MKG Consulting ranked the 20 largest, worldwide hotel brands by rooms for 2004 as follows:

1. Best Western 310,245
2. Holiday Inn 287,769
3. Comfort Inns & Suites 177,444
4. Marriott 173,974
5. Days Inn 157,995
6. Sheraton 134,648
7. Hampton Inn 127,543
8. Super 8 126,421
9. Holiday Inn Express 120,296
10. Ramada 104,636
11. Radisson 103,709
12. Motel 6 92,468
13. Quality Inns 92,011
14. Hyatt 89,602
15. Hilton 89,012
16. Courtyard 88,214
17. Mercure 86,239
18. Hilton Int'l 73,058
19. Ibis 69,950
20. Novotel 67,268

friendly, or even parking friendly if those issues are important to you. An appealing option in many areas is locally called the Park n' Fly. Smaller hotels and motels in the vicinity of the airport are offering parking for little more than the cost of one night's room. The participating hotel or motel generally must have a large parking lot and will issue a parking permit that stays inside the car for the period of time that you will be away. The rates are similar to, or lower than, the airport's

World-Famous Hotels

Atlantis Paradise Is. .... Bahamas
Balmoral Hotel .... Edinburgh
Beverly Hills Hotel .... California
Caesar Park Hotel .... Buenos Aires
Copacabana Palace .... Rio de Janeiro
Corinthia Grand .... Budapest
Dar Masyaf .... Dubai
Four Seasons .... Istanbul
Golden Tulip .... Jerusalem
Grand Hotel Plaza .... Rome
Grand Hotel .... Beijing
Grand Hyatt (tallest) .... Shanghai
Grand Hyatt .... Singapore
Grotta Giusta .... Tuscany
Hay-Adams Hotel .... Washington, D.C.
Hotel Adlon .... Berlin
Hotel Danieli .... Venice
Hotel de Crillon .... Paris
Hotel del Coronado .... San Diego
Hotel Nacional .... Havana
Hotel Ritz.. Madrid
Hotel Sacher .... Vienna
Intercontinental .... Paris
King David Hotel .... Israel
Las Brisas .... Acapulco
Lloyd Hotel... Amsterdam
Makati Shangri-La .... Manila
Mark Hopkins .... San Francisco
Mena House Oberoi .... Cairo
MGM Grand .... Las Vegas
Peninsula Hong Kong .... China
President and Casino .... Prague
Royal Hawaiian .... Honolulu
Shangri-La Hotel .... Kuala Lumpur
Taj Mahal Hotel .... India
The Drake Hotel .... Chicago
The Empress .... Victoria, B.C.
The Imperial .... New Delhi
The National Hotel .... Miami
The Oriental .... Bangkok
The Ritz Hotel .... London
The Westin .... Sydney
Waldorf-Astoria .... New York City

long-term parking rates. The advantage is you get one good night's rest, are close to the airport, and shuttled to the airport at the appropriate time.

Hotel Reliability, Comfort, and Price

If in doubt about what hotel to choose at a new destination, there is much to be said for the extremely large hotel chains that provide a high or very high level of service with great consistency and reliability every day of every year. You will likely know what to expect and at least meet your expectations when you stay at one of their properties. In return, you can typically expect to pay

somewhat of a premium price in exchange for the assurances that the property will be clean, safe, secure, updated, well managed, and will have at least the minimum of quality amenities and services that you anticipate. Due to size and brand recognition, however, there may be less potential to negotiate a more favorable price such as there is with the independent, small, and less familiar properties that must also compete with the corporate giants. Super 8 Hotels/Motels, for instance, are well known, a large chain of properties, and already priced in the budget market. By knowing what the "biggest and most reliable" hotels would charge for given nights,

you will have a good benchmark for what may be realistic to pay at a small property that may not be as favorably located. Also, unless the hotel is a major focal point of your journey, do you want to pay for amenities that you do not intend to use? Also consider child-friendly and/or pet-friendly condominium properties as another alternative. If you are looking for unique, national flavor that is not the homogenized approach to temporary housing, consider doing more research for the boutique hotels and bed-and-breakfast properties that usually offer an entirely different and likely far more memorable experience. It is all about choices.

And Now for the Winners!

A reader's poll of *Travel Weekly Magazine* (January 16, 2006) produced the following hotel property winners:

• **Ritz-Carlton**, headquartered in Chevy Chase, MD (www.ritzcarlton.com) was voted the most luxurious hotel chain in the world for the third consecutive year.

• **Four Seasons Hotel** (www.fourseasons.com) is headquartered in Toronto and repeated last year's position as the number one chain in the international category.

• **InterContinental Hotels & Resorts** which is described as having 136 properties and is headquartered in Windsor, England (www.ichotelsgroup.com) was voted the best European hotel for 2005.

• **Sandals Resorts of Miami, Florida** (www.sandals.com) has 12 couples-only, all-inclusive resorts and was voted the best in the Caribbean for the third straight year.

• **Marriott Hotels and Resorts**, a branch of Marriott International (www.marriott.com) was voted the best domestic hotel chain for the second year in a row.

• **Hampton Inn**, headquartered in Beverly Hills, California (www.hamptoninn.com) was voted into first place among the economy hotel chains.

Additional Sources of Information

www.abba.com
www.ase.net/reviews.html
www.bedandbreakfast.com
www.beststay.com
www.bhrc.co.uk
www.calibex.com
www.choicehotels.com
www.epinions.com/hotels
www.fodors.com/reviews
www.hostelz.com
www.hotelchatter.com

www.hotelmotelreviews.com
www.hotelshark.com
www.hoteltravelcheck.com
www.hotelwatchdog.com
www.mytravelguide.com
www.redweek.com
www.travelpost.com
www.tripconnect.com
www.vacationspot.com
www.women-traveling.com
www.zoomandgo.com

13
Traveling Solo

The man who goes alone can start today, but he who travels with another must wait till that other is ready.

—Henry David Thoreau

The Challenge of Traveling Alone

One of the most challenging issues is the need to make most or all of the decisions yourself. You may need to gather all of the details, buy a plane ticket, decide what to wear, and make all reservations. You may need to make all meal arrangements, arrange for transfers (connections), roll your own bags, and quickly get to know a lot of new places and people. Actually, the whole process can be very gratifying when you take away worries about forgetting or doing something wrong, making decisions too quickly, and somehow looking "foolish." For one thing, you will not have to coordinate with one or more other travelers on each and every detail. You can slow down the process, if desired, and savor the details that are relevant only to you.

Anticipation of the journey is one of the major rewards and becomes a part of establishing your independence as a competent traveler. You can expect to learn as you go as every last detail can never be anticipated. You can expect to be sharing your time with others and to explore likes and dislikes without dragging along a travel partner who just doesn't see things the same way.

Travel Reminders

- Make sure you have a signed, valid passport and visas, if required.
- Watch for U.S. government travel warnings for countries you plan to visit.
- Have an emergency plan. Keep all important numbers in a separate place.
- Confirm your medical insurance. Medicare is not valid outside of the U.S.
- Be attentive to local laws and customs and avoid overly familiar "Good Samaritans."
- Avoid accepting help with your luggage or packages from strangers.
- Avoid telling anyone who does not need to know that you are traveling alone.
- Avoid conspicuous clothing, expensive-looking jewelry, or large amounts of cash.
- Ask for directions before you leave your hotel. Ask the hotel to call a taxi for you.
- Ensure that your hotel has good security and easy access to transportation.
- Trust your instincts. Be especially observant of anything that seems not right.
- Be positive, purposeful, out-going, and have a really great experience.

Independent travelers going solo typically get readily involved with new cultures, quickly make new friends, and get a great sense of personal satisfaction from the experience. On April 26, 2005, *USA Today* reporter Susan Bowles wrote, "According to the Department of Commerce's office of Travel and Tourism Industries, 41% of the almost 24.5 million people who traveled abroad in 2003 ... went solo." That is a lot of happy and confident travelers.

Minors Traveling Alone

Traveling alone as a minor can produce different issues. Generally, airlines must be consulted in advance and will likely have distinct guidelines to be followed. It's also common to have an additional airline fee to provide "child watch services." Another alternative is to pay an attendant to accompany the child and to ensure that appropriate connections with responsible adults are completed. Continental Airlines, for example, considers children in the age range of 5 to 14 years to be unaccompanied minors when not with at least one responsible companion who is at least 18 years of age. If requested by the parents, adolescents between the ages of 15 and 17 may be classified as "minors." Children under 5 years of age are not allowed to fly alone on Continental. Allowed children under the age of 8 years are accepted for nonstop and direct flights only. Alaska Airlines' "Unaccompanied Minor Service" is very similar and is available for children from 5 to 17 years of age on both domestic and international flights. Specific details should always be verified in advance and preferably by telephone rather than the Internet and with the specific airline being considered.

Single Supplement

The term "single supplement" is well known to travel consultants and to many seasoned travelers throughout the world who travel alone. The term refers to the single traveler and is typically associated with the higher unit cost for cruises and tours. The basic economical rule behind this particular disadvantage relates to basic supply and demand. Example: If a cruise with 300 cabins agreed to single occupancy for a group of 300 singles, there

Suggestions for Women Traveling Alone

- Consider gender-friendly hotel rooms that provide a hair dryer, perhaps an iron, and are not in isolated locations.

- Consider properties with kitchenettes to save money and to avoid eating in restaurants for each meal. Individually owned and small hotel/motel properties may offer this feature to help improve their competitiveness. Major hotel chains such as Hilton, Marriott, and Sheraton are not likely to have such options. Some travel companies have special promotions for the single traveler. Your personal travel consultant can typically be very helpful in assisting you to find what you need.

- Creatively avoid peak travel times to the extent possible and get more for your money and lessen the chance of being "swallowed up" in enormous crowds.

- Seek the best price and do what you can to negotiate or eliminate the single supplement charge that might otherwise be imposed for a cruise or tour.

- Consider starting with local attractions, long-weekend trips to help establish the style and means of travel you prefer before committing to a foreign venture of many weeks that doesn't fit well with your particular lifestyle.

- Consider additional references that cater to the solo female traveler by carefully surfing the web, reading travel magazines, and travel books. Ask lots of questions and insist on good answers.

would be a distinct loss of income compared to renting most cabins for double, triple, or quad occupancy. The compromise is to set most cruise and tour prices as "per person double occupancy (ppdo)." The single supplement portion is the adjusted cost for a solitary person only that is above the per person price quoted if two or more persons were to occupy the same space. It is comparable to a penalty or surcharge for traveling alone instead of being a group of two or more persons traveling in a cruise cabin, or tour.

Various "solutions" to avoid the extra cost of a single supplement include agreeing in advance to be pooled with a travel companion (a "share"), or to find such a party in advance. It can be a great time to consider traveling as a parent and child, brother and sister, two or more friends, or any combination greater than the number one.

Seniors Traveling Solo

Author and columnist, Tom Blake, describes his book, *Finding Love After 50: How to Begin. Where to Go. What to Do*,

as follows: *"Finding Love After 50* is the only dating book written by a man exclusively for the 29 million singles age 50 and older that shows them how to find love. Widowed and divorced singles will learn how to overcome loneliness, make themselves desirable, discover places to go to meet other eligible singles, and optimize their chances of meeting a compatible mate. There's someone out there for everyone; this book will help bring them together." For additional details see www.findingloveafter50.com/travel.

Additional Sources of Information

www.airsafe.com/kidsafe
www.committment.com
www.cstn.org
www.roadtripamerica.com
www.solosingles.com
www.tangodiva.com

www.trafalgar.com
www.transitionsabroad.com
www.travelaloneandloveit.com
www.travelcompanions.com
www.travelsense.org
www.womens-tours.com

14
Travel with Children

All kids need is a little help, a little hope, and somebody who believes in them. —Earvin "Magic" Johnson

Plan with the Kids, Not for Them

Include your children in the family's vacation planning. This includes where to go as well as how to entertain themselves while in transit from Point A to Point B. Assisting children with choices and decisions that they can understand and be a part of will likely enhance the total experience. It can be helpful to agree on games

(electronic and others), word puzzles, mind-challenging activities, drawing materials, and solicit ideas from your children to help create entertaining challenges. The goal is ideally to do much more than just fill their time. It is an opportunity to build on family togetherness and play out the give and take that can have meaning for other parts of their lives. Making a game of the travel experience itself can be rewarding to all. A trip doesn't have to be educational or enlightening in any formal sense, but in many ways it typically turns out that way without having to even comment on it. Added structure (interactive games) helps to break the monotony of travel, which can be far more intense for a child than it is for an adult, especially if the child was not thrilled about going. The energy level of children is typically far greater than for adults and kids tend to focus on the here and now more than abstract notions about the value of a vacation.

High Energy Doesn't Have to Be a Liability

Attention spans and focus for adults and children will almost always be different and perhaps radically different. This is especially true when confined to the tight parameters of a car, plane, ship, or train for any amount of time. Just getting children to consider changing their present agenda to what you have in mind is quite a challenge. It is tough leaving the neighborhood friends behind, maybe disrupting school, and maybe just leaving a comfort zone for what may be an adult-oriented activity. One remedy is to obtain travel magazine and online reviews about the programs that are available for kids.

Children's Programs

Aboard cruise ships that cater to a younger population and that are receptive to children, the programs available for them are exciting, activity-oriented, both entertainment and education-oriented, well supervised, and typically much more appealing to the children than the adult-only activities would be. Children's programs are usually age-graded. This allows children to be with others their age and to participate in activities appropriate to their level of maturity. The availability of good programs specifically for children should be confirmed before booking. A room or two that is set aside for children to be on their own is not a program. Get your questions answered in advance by the source and consider looking at online reviews of the program before making a commitment. Your travel consultant may also be able to help in finding good activities and programs for children. Reading reviews of kid's programs is probably the ideal way to make some determinations about the program. Then discuss the possibilities with your children.

Memorable Experiences for Children

Prior to the ages of 6, 7, or 8 years, long-term travel memories are mostly non-verbal images that may be difficult to recall later in life. The early childhood encounters with real people and diverse places, however, are still likely to make very favorable impressions that will last for a long time. Children of all ages are able to expand their "world view" through travel experiences that are vivid, first-hand, and revealing in ways that television cartoons and video games cannot match. Children who observe other people first-hand during their vacation travel are likely to gain from the experience in ways that are different from textbook educations.

Some children may need the assistance of very structured kids' programs that are appropriate to their age group. Others, especially teenagers, may quickly get to know others near their own age and form lasting friendships that reach out well beyond the neighborhood kids back home. See Chapter 16 on amusement parks and theme parks.

Travel with School-Age Children

One way to enhance a vacation travel experience is to speak to the child's teacher well in advance to get feedback about the kind of experience that might be of most interest or most educational value. It is possible that a teacher may incorporate details about a particular destination as a classroom project, or perhaps as an individual project for your child (or children). Special attention could be given to the cultural similarities and differences of the people that they may be visiting. Attention could be given to geographical differences and other factors such as customs, language, history, folklore, music, art, and even how schools in the visited country are similar and dissimilar.

It can be an opportunity to stress the importance of having and showing their identification when requested by others. Additional behaviors to encourage could be staying with the group, being polite and respectful as the guest in another country, and keeping in touch by cell phone or other means throughout the full itinerary of the trip. It can be an experience in managing their money, making purchases in a different setting, and for relating constructive stories of their experiences to friends and classmates when they return. Taking their own photographs, with permission in some instances such as churches and government buildings, can add to their narrative and their memories when they get back home.

Just seeing how their peers do some things in the same way and other things in distinctly different ways can help to give a different perspective to their own lives. School children in many foreign countries, for instance, wear uniforms and must attain certain levels of proficiency in different subjects to continue with their formal education. Example: Scandinavian children have the

123

basics of their college education paid by the government if they qualify academically. Some children must help the family financially or perhaps commit some time for military service after completing their school experience. Actually seeing differences helps to communicate that alternate ways of doing things are not absolutely right or wrong, just different. A vacation for and with children can be far more than a good time. Vacation travel is education for life.

Sample Activities and Programs to Interest Children

Amusement parks
Aquariums
Arts, sports, and special needs
Babar's World Tour book
Beaches and pools
Campground
Child-inspired travel
Children's programs, plays
Children's Museums
Christmas markets
Club Med family vacations
Cruise ship kids' programs

Cultural experiences
Educational experiences
Family car travel
NASA space tours
National Parks
Playgrounds
Puzzle Map of Europe
School holiday travel
Theme parks
Travel for teens
Whale-watching
Zoos and animal parks

Additional Sources of Information

www.adventureteentravel.com
www.americanhistory.si.edu
www.babiestravellite.com
www.consumerreports.org
www.disneyland.com
www.disneyworld.com
www.essortment.com
www.familyonboard.com
www.familytravelforum.com
www.familytravelguides.com
www.flyingwithkids.com
www.freetraveltips.com/kids

www.iloveny.com/kids
www.kidsdomain.com
www.madallie.com
www.mytravelguide.com
www.nationalgeographic.com
www.nycvisit.com
www.onestepahead.com
www.passporthealthusa.com
www.transitionsabroad.com
www.travelingwithchildren.co.uk
www.travelwithkids.about.com

15
Travel with Pets

I like pigs. Dogs look up to us. Cats look down on us.
Pigs treat us as equals. —Winston Churchill

Confirm First, Then Go

The single most important consideration in traveling with a pet is to call ahead and confirm that your pet(s) will be allowed and under what conditions. There is always the potential that there has been a management change or ownership change and distinctly new rules or policies may be in place. Checking on Internet websites alone may not be sufficiently current. Another consideration is to check on the costs involved. Resources for travelers with pets are becoming more common and friendlier but acceptance in one place can be very different from others. Many hotel/motel managements have pet bans in place or are very restrictive with respect to type, size, and perhaps other factors.

Pets Traveling Alone

If flying with NWA, contact Northwest Cargo, for instance, at 1-800-692-2746, or www.NWA.com/travel/animals at least five hours in advance for intended same-day live shipment (not as cargo).

Service is available at all U.S. airports served by Northwest Airlines. Pricing and other specifics should be available online, but direct contact with the airline is definitely recommended before final plans for shipment of a pet are made. If a pet is to be shipped by air, make all arrangements well in advance. Follow the airline instructions carefully and be very certain that a responsible person will be at the destination at the right times and in the right place to receive the pet. Give that person the flight number and air freight identification numbers by phone before leaving the airport. If the pet is not picked up as agreed, you might incur a charge for boarding the pet.

Pet Travel Stress

If you must travel with a pet(s), consider that travel can be unusually stressful for pets as they are suddenly out of their comfort zones. Anticipate a greater need for leashes as the stressed pet may suddenly run off and be difficult or impossible to retrieve. "Accidents" are more likely to occur on the floor due to stress. Plastic zip-lock bags and some tissue paper will help to correct most situations. Cats are especially prone to suddenly running off the moment a car door is opened and can be very difficult to recover.

Pets Left at Home

Consider a trusted pet-sitter who will care for your pet in much the same manner that you would do yourself and for an agreed price, a nice gift that you will bring back, or perhaps a reciprocity plan to care for their pet during their travel or emergencies. Another alternative is to consider a kennel service that is provided by a veterinarian or a private business that cares for animals and that you have carefully inspected.

Special Pet Carriers

Buses and trains, in particular, may allow the transport of small dogs and cats in approved pet carriers. Be sure your pet is not susceptible to car sickness. In some instances a veterinarian can suggest travel sickness or mild sedation medications. Making water available is another major consideration.

Call the Foreign Consulate

Contact the consulate office of a foreign country to be visited. Mexico, for instance, allows dogs and cats as the only pets that may be brought into that country. Get all of the specifics in advance. Exotic and unusual pets (birds, ferrets, lizards, mice, rats, hamsters, guinea pigs, insects, turtles, snakes, formerly wild animals, alligators, iguanas, horses, domestic animals and others) will likely be restricted or banned in most places and may lead to substantial fines or confiscation of the pet due to legal bans and/or the possible transfer of disease.

Pet Identification

When a pet travels with you, be sure that identification is valid for where you can be reached at the moment (e.g., cell phone number) and a back-up person who can authorize details for the pet's care, return to owner, and pay expenses that may be involved. An implanted I.D. microchip that is put in place by a veterinarian is one of the very best means of finding and recovering a lost pet.

Specially Trained Dogs

Seeing-eye dogs who accompany a visually impaired person will typically be allowed to travel or reside at a particular property even when pets are typically excluded. The same may be true for other animals that have been specially trained to assist someone with a disability. The important factor is to confirm all details in advance. Instead of a dispute with the management, consider rewarding the pet-friendly sources with your travel dollars.

Vaccination Records

It may be necessary to present records of current shots for rabies, licensing, and possible details for a microchip that may be in use for identification as well. If there is any visible evidence of health problems, the pet may be rejected for transport and not allowed exposure to other pets.

Not Without My Pet

The importance of pets was underscored once again when Hurricane Katrina struck New Orleans in September, 2005. Many residents who remained in their homes with their pets soon needed to be rescued themselves but refused to board buses when they were informed that they could not bring their pets. Not too surprisingly, the bond between humans and pets is all but unbreakable.

Five-Star Alternatives

A little reasonable search in advance usually produces very acceptable hotels that will allow pets (especially smaller pets). Some 5-star properties that don't allow pets on the premises may offer a neighboring facility where the pet can stay for a modest price. Daily contact with the pet can then be maintained.

A Growing Trend

It has been estimated that up to one-quarter of U.S. and Canadian travelers take a pet along on their vacation each year and that number is increasing. The most obvious solution is to take a pet in the family car (SUV, RV, motorhome, etc.). Virgin Atlantic Airlines, for instance, has started to issue pet passports for positive identification during air travel. Northwest Airlines offers live shipment of pets.

Pet-Friendly Travel Consultants

Internet search for pet-friendly vendors of all types is far more simplified than it once was. It is also much easier to find a knowledgeable and pet-friendly travel consultant. Professional travel consultants can also be helpful in obtaining reliable information about international pet laws and customs and possible quarantine requirements. Such information may include the specifics of allowed pet containers, food and water dispensers, and how to deal with required vaccinations (or vaccination records), pet droppings, and possible illness or injury.

Each Locality Is a Little Different

Each city, state, and each area of each country will have its own specific laws, rules, or customs relating to pets. Some areas have very specific leash laws (some areas are even set aside as leash-free zones). Regulations may also vary at beaches, parks, sidewalks, and business properties. Clearly, some areas are more pet-friendly than others and the trend is improving in most but not all areas.

Cruise with Pet

The Cunard cruise ship, HMS Queen Mary 2 (QM2), which is 1,132-feet in length and launched in 2004, actually has a pet kennel on board. Located on Deck 12, the pet facility even has a designated kennel master.

Suggested Pet-Friendly Resources

www.animalfair.com   www.pethealthcare.co.uk
www.dogfriendly.com   www.petsonthego.com
www.doglogic.com   www.pettravel.com
www.healthypet.com   www.petvacations.com
www.i-pets.com   www.takeyourpet.com
www.jet-a-pet.com   www.thepetproject.com
www.letsgopets.com   www.travelingdogs.com
www.petcareinsurance.com   www.travelpets.com
www.petfriendlytravel.com   www.tripswithpets.com

16
Amusement and Theme Parks

A child on a farm sees a plane fly by overhead and dreams of a faraway place. A traveler on the plane sees the farmhouse and dreams of home. —Carl Burns

Amusement and Theme Parks in General

Children, teenagers, adults of all ages, and grandparents all contribute, in their own way, to be the driving force that sustains major amusement parks. Walt Disney, for example, is understood to have acquired the inspiration for a mega-amusement park after taking his daughters for rides on the carousel at Griffith Park in Los Angeles. His dream included magical story-book themes and exciting activities that would focus on children but have appeal for all ages. His energy and vision has been kept alive with unbelievable investments of creativity, money, and attentiveness to the new themes that continue to evolve. Disney films that introduce whole new families of characters and imaginative settings also introduce new toys, games, DVDs, and even the music that young children will incorporate in their lives. Each blockbuster series of films, such as *Lord of the Rings, Harry Potter,* and *Spiderman,* introduces whole new worlds of possibilities for children's imaginations and consumer wants. In such a carefully orchestrated environment, an older theme, such as Charles Schultz's *Peanuts* characters of Charlie Brown, Snoopy, and Lucy, becomes passé. Old West characters such as Roy Rogers, Gene Autry, and Hopalong Cassidy can be a faint or even non-existent memory among adults now entering middle age. Parks that relate best to their changing young audiences have the best chances to prosper and grow.

Entertainment parks for both children and adults have a long and colorful history that dates back to Bakken Theme Park in Klampenborg, Denmark, in the 1500s. The overall trend in recent times has been for the relatively unique and isolated theme parks to be overtaken by huge amusement parks in high population areas with access to an international airport and lots of hotel and motel space both near and on the park property. In the early 1950s, Walt Disney went a long way to help perfect the model for the mega-amusement park with unique features that would reach out to children and adults of all ages. Along with increasing size and popularity, amusement parks have become major profit centers for food, housing, transportation, souvenirs, and entertainment. Vast promotional effort is continuously made to make the park experience enticing, memorable, and as all-inclusive as possible once on the property. Surprisingly, a great many of the hundreds of millions of visitors each year tend to overlook the reality that a season pass may be just a few dollars more than the price of a one-day visit. Also, coping with large numbers of people and long lines (queues) play an important part in the experience and requires assertive creativity to get gate passes, housing, parking, and even good access to the special features that were the original attraction.

Sampling of U.S. and Int'l Amusement and Theme Parks
Astroland Amusement Park, Coney Island, NY
Bakken, Klampenborg, Denmark (oldest)
Busch Gardens, Orlando, FL
Castle Park, Riverside, CA

Cedar Point Amusement Park, Sandusky, OH
Disney World, Orlando, FL
Disneyland Resort, Paris, FR
Disneyland, Anaheim, CA
Disneyland, Tokyo, Japan (most visited)
Dreamworld, Coomera, Queensland, Australia
Everland, Kyonggi-Do, So. Korea
Florida Aquarium, Tampa, FL
Hershey Park, Hershey, PA
Kennedy Space Center, Orlando, FL
Kennywood Amusement Park, West Mifflin, PA
Knoebels Amusement Resort, Elysburg, PA
Knott's Berry Farm, Anaheim, CA
Legoland, San Diego, CA
Mystery Park, Interlaken, Switzerland
Parrot Jungle Island, Miami, FL
Playland Park, Rye, NY
Quassy Amusement Park, Middlebury, CT
Ratanga Junction, near Cape Town, So. Africa
Seabreeze Amusement Park, Rochester, NY
Sesame Place, Langhome, PA
Six Flags Parks (31) in USA and one in Mexico
Universal Studios, Hollywood, CA

A Sampling of Southern California Parks
• Disneyland/California Adventure Park
The following are extracts of the experiences of a family of four (including the writer's grandsons, ages 7 and 10) who visited multiple parks during the Christmas season, 2005. The first observation was that everyone was apparently at Disneyland (December 23, 24, and 25) because the other parks were relatively empty. California Adventure Park is actually across the street from Disneyland. It is owned by Disney but focuses more on Disney movie themes such as *A Bug's Life, Monsters, Inc.,* and others. This family had a CityPass (see: www.citypass.com) which included a Disneyland Resort Park Hopper ticket good for three days with one day of early admission to Disneyland. A CityPass can be

purchased online at the site indicated or at participating retailers such as Costco, and included admittance to several different theme parks.

Disneyland opened at 8 a.m.; the family arrived at 7 a.m. and was able to use the one-time early admission feature of the Park  Pass. The children were able to take six different rides in that first hour because the park was not very busy. During the rest of the day, the two boys were able to accelerate the ride process because of Disney's "Fast Pass" system. The purpose of the Fast Pass is to save a visitor's place in a long line so other portions of the park can be enjoyed without repeatedly spending long periods of time standing in each line. Both Disneyland and California Adventure make use of the Fast Pass system to expedite reservations for rides (note: not every ride has this feature, but most of the new rides do). The ParkPass (Hopper) is inserted into a Fast Pass machine for the desired ride, and you receive a reservation that is good for a one-hour block of time to return, walk to the head of the line, and get right on the ride. This can only be done for one reservation at a time and you cannot use it again until your reservation for the previous Fast Pass expires.

Since it was Disneyland's fiftieth anniversary, and it was the Christmas season, acres and acres of landscaped grounds were decked out with wonderful decorations commemorating both occasions. The ride called "It's a Small World" had a song mix of "It's a Small World" combined with "Jingle Bells" and "Deck the Halls." The crowds were huge, but it was still lots of fun, and considered well worth the cost. Another example of the value received is that Disneyland is constantly evolving. As a result of new Disney movies, many of the newer rides and attractions are named after these popularized themes. The dated submarine ride known as "20,000 Leagues Under the Sea" is now being refurbished and will soon be the "Finding Nemo" submarine ride. The Haunted House has been changed and is now themed after "The Nightmare Before Christmas."

For obvious reasons, children who repeatedly watch DVDs of popular movies that are oriented for their age group *really know* the look and feel of those characters and themes. The Disney people are very serious about relating to both traditional and contemporary themes that they exhaustively promote. It is the major way that they sustain interest and continues to bring in new audiences by the millions. Many of the details for park use, hotels, meals, and transportation have become so complex that entire books are written on the subject such as: *Disneyland & Southern California with Kids,* by Michael and Trisha Knight. Having the "best time at the best price" at theme parks is now so complex and subject to change that reading a book specifically on that park is recommended in addition to Internet search and use of a travel agent who specializes in theme parks.

• Legoland
In keeping with the Lego theme, Legoland Park in San Diego is divided into nine distinct "blocks." There are shops and restaurants within two of the blocks (The Beginning and The Garden). Other blocks contain stunning Lego exhibits, rides, and activities to involve children "of all ages." The Castle Hill Block includes a medieval theme with castle, the Dragon, and

Merlin the Magician. Two different roller coaster rides are also located within that block. A jungle gym castle has towers, slides, and catwalks that can be climbed. Very young children can play with actual Legos as the older children are more actively occupied with certain rides or exhibits that better match their age level. In addition to the various themes are the several shows throughout the park that are sure to be of interest to children.

Be sure to confirm the admission price as a part of your preliminary planning. At the end of 2005 the admission price for a family of four was just under $200 and was not included in the CityPass. The theme park is very interesting, at times dazzling, and seriously recommended for children and adults of all ages. There are incredible Lego structures such as replicas of several cities, imaginative critters, and objects on a scale that is truly stunning considering the humble size and design of a specific Lego piece. The experience does include rides that may be best for younger children. The park should be appealing to any children with a special interest in Legos. My grandsons rated the visit to Legoland above the visit to the San Diego Zoo. It is recommended that first-time visitors seek discount coupons for the park admission passes and pack a lunch. The prices of food and drinks at the park were found to be well above comparable products at movie theaters. The overall experience was very favorable.

• Knott's Berry Farm

This theme park is on the must-do list of most travelers who want to experience Southern California's major attractions and was included in the 2005 CityPass, but not 2006. It is described as "America's First Theme Park," and is well located in a sunshine-oriented playground of the state. The present irony, however, is that the park relies heavily on the Peanuts theme of Snoopy, Charlie Brown, and other animated characters created by Charles Schultz many years ago. Early elementary-age children will likely recognize Charlie Brown and Snoopy, but the supporting characters are becoming difficult for young children to recognize. The park does have some thrill rides such as a fast-start roller coaster and a free-fall drop ride. Knott's Berry Farm appears to lack the fascination that young children now have for entirely different super-heroes and newer animated characters that are in critical demand. The Southern California CityPass may be shifted from Knott's Berry Farm to Universal Studios of Hollywood effective in 2006. Be sure to verify with www.citypass.com and also consider CityPass admissions for cities outside of Southern California.

• SeaWorld
This world-famous park attracts guests from virtually every part of the world and is also a part of the Anheuser-Busch park system. One of the extra amenities of that particular connection is the opportunity to see the West Coast Clydesdale Horses. Like Legoland, the admission price at the gate can be a shocker but it is included in the CityPass. SeaWorld is a great mix of attractions,

shows, exhibits, rides, and sights to please everyone. The star attraction is *Shamu*, the world famous killer whale. The whale may actually be a replacement for the original but is always a great crowd pleaser. The killer whales and dolphins performing in unison are something that you must see in person to really appreciate. The park is a consistent crowd pleaser for all ages, but it does not include high-adrenaline thrill-rides.

• San Diego Zoo
The ideal weather of San Diego contributes substantially to the activity level of animals on exhibit in naturalistic settings. It is probably the world's best-rated and most-visited zoo for those reasons and more. You will need to follow maps and to allow

plenty of time to realistically see all of the zoo's diversity. The general rule at present is that it may be a 90-minute wait to see the baby panda bear, but at times there is no waiting at all. The well-identified flora and fauna that grow so well in that climate is also well worth taking the time to notice, and to photograph. Anticipate spending a full day of viewing to enjoy all that the zoo has to offer. It also pays to get an early start on your day. Incidentally, there is a plaque at the Seattle (Washington) Zoo that shows a bell curve distribution of animal activity and visitor activity. The two different curves barely overlap. The point of the story is that most zoo animal activity is greatest in the early and cooler part of the day and visitor activity is greatest in the warmer and later part of the day. Have you ever wondered why the bears and tigers seem to sleep so much during the warm afternoons?

Additional Sources of Information

www.123world.com/amusement
www.aaa.com
www.aerospacemuseum.org
www.autry-museum.org
www.catalinainfo.com
www.citypass.com
www.disneylandparis.com
www.disneyworld.com
www.funguide.com
www.getty.edu
www.googlesightseeing.com
www.hollywoodmuseum.com
www.iaapa.org
www.interthemepark.com

www.lazoo.org
www.medievaltimes.com
www.mouseplanet.com
www.mtr.org
www.nhm.org
www.queenmary.com
www.rhfleet.org
www.sandiegozoo.org
www.sdnhm.org
www.seaworld.com
www.sixflags.com
www.tarpits.org
www.viator.com
www.yesterland.com

17
Travel with Disabilities

*For my part, I travel not to go anywhere, but to go. I
travel for travel's sake, the great affair is to move.*
— Robert Louis Stevenson

Mobility Is a Primary Travel Concern

Accommodation for disabled travelers throughout most of the
best-traveled destinations around the world continues to improve.
The economic incentive to accommodate all travelers is a force
that cannot be denied. Travel, the world's largest and fastest-
growing industry is all about people of every description mingling,
dining, shopping, sleeping, and experiencing new destinations in a
very positive way. The image of a traveler with disabilities,
however, is typically that of the wheelchair-bound individual.
Disabled parking areas in the U.S., for example, are usually marked
with the graphic symbol of a person in a wheelchair and the space
is supposed to allow for wheelchair maneuverability. However,
the majority of people who obtain disabled parking permits from
their doctor have health and mobility concerns, but are not confined
to a wheelchair. Individual mobility is the issue for active travel
and adaptations can often be made, but not always. For those truly
in need of a wheelchair, there are many variations ranging from
the cutaway models used by athletes in competitive events to the
completely powered chairs used by quadriplegics such as world-
famous scientist, Stephen Hawking, author of *The Universe in a
Nutshell* and other books. Travel requires mobility and there will
always be variations in each individual's physical mobility.

ADA Is Not the Law Outside of the U.S.

In the United States, substantial attention has been given to
architectural accessibility and related issues following the passage
of the Department of Labor's Americans with Disabilities Act
(effective July 26, 1992). The basic purpose of the law is to create
"a more level playing field" for all persons regardless of disability

and mobility issues. Where possible, new construction must facilitate access with such features as sidewalk curb-cuts, ramps, railings, wider and easier-to-use doors, elevators, and accessible bathrooms. Older buildings are likewise expected to include accessibility retrofits as a condition of approval for remodeling. Although the law relates to the United States, the intent within the law has been acknowledged in most of the tourist-oriented parts of the world. The primary exceptions are the old, historic parts of Europe and Asia where streets are very narrow, sidewalks irregular, and stairs required for just about every public access. Curbs often do not have curb-cuts, cobblestone streets can be very uneven and perhaps steep, and areas of grossly deferred maintenance or construction projects can be worse.

The recommended way to evaluate accessibility issues in specific locations outside of the U.S. is to read reviews written by travelers who have recently returned from the area of your interest.

On June 6, 2005, the U.S. Supreme Court published a decision in reference to the Americans with Disabilities Act and cruise ships. The case was called Spector v. NCL and the court's ruling was that the ADA does apply to foreign flagged cruise ships that call on U.S. ports. The decision, it is understood, does not require the removal of all barriers on all ships. Justice Anthony Kennedy indicated that structural changes must be achievable yet not alter a ship's design, or threaten the safety of passengers and crew. Much of the original concern was with the older ships. Newer ship designs usually incorporate as many accessibility features as passenger safety and ship function will allow. Ultimately, as people throughout the world extend their life spans, improving accessibility is potentially a major benefit to everyone.

Mobility Impairments
There may be major distinctions between mobility with a collapsible, manual wheelchair and a relatively heavy power wheelchair. Fortunately, there have been great reductions in the size and weight of many powered chairs and a great many van and small bus transport services have become available in larger cities.

140

Careful research should be done well in advance of each travel plan to be certain that accessibility can be accommodated. Much depends on the ability to do transfers, or to use a walker briefly, or to have the assistance of one or more attendants. Other mobility issues can be assisted with a cane, quad cane, crutches, walking stick, cane with a built-in seat, Canadian crutches, orthopedic braces, and a variety of different styled walkers.

Visual Impairments

Persons who are substantially visually impaired, legally blind, or totally blind may extend their travel independence with careful travel reviews in advance to verify the suitability of resources at different travel destinations. For some, a telescoping white cane with red tip for coping with uneven surfaces, stairs, and obstructions, projects a non-verbal image to others that the person with the white cane is attempting to be as independent as possible. Additional assistance can include electronic sensors, a guide dog, very dark glasses, and in some instances an attendant. With partial sight it may be possible to read menus and other printed materials with a hand-held magnifying glass with its own light. A travel companion or spouse may also be very helpful in extending the range for the visually impaired traveler.

Hearing Impairments

Total deafness may restrict communication with officials and others to written messages or perhaps the use of a translator who can communicate in sign language (Amslan). Many hearing impairments are facilitated with improved versions of hearing aids and may not represent a significant impairment for travel. Getting and understanding directions, in some instances, might be a bit more difficult but an extra bit of effort will likely get the traveler wherever he/she wants to go without unusual duress. The TDD/TYY telephone system and text messaging with cell phones can also assist travelers with a hearing impairment.

Size Matters

Some adults and many child travelers are too small for their feet to touch the floor when seated on commercial airplanes, buses, cars, and other conveyances that are typically designed for the "average person." Very tall people, for instance, may experience some discomfort or at least inconvenience with low doorways, short beds, rental equipment in the wrong size, and even hard-to-find replacement clothing. The extremely large person may not be able to fit in an airline seat that has non-moveable arms. In some instances it's necessary to fly business or first class or even pay for two seats rather than one for all connections. If an extremely large person is also having mobility limitations, the need for special assistance and advance research is even more important.

Developmental Disabilities

Any limitation that has been present since birth or due to slow onset is very much a known factor and will be an additional factor to consider in travel planning. The family member with mental disabilities may need the assistance of other family or travel group members to assure their ability to enjoy all of the positives of travel without the inconvenience of getting lost, or inability to make all necessary connections, business arrangements, and financial transactions necessary to complete recreational travel. To some extent, a phobia has many of the characteristics of a developmental disability. Acrophobia (the fear of falling) can be very inhibiting if severe and may limit some aspects of a travel plan. Seasickness or fear of flying may be a reality from past experience, but tends to also have a phobic quality about it. Gosh, maybe the plane will crash or the ship will sink. There simply are no absolute guarantees but the public safety record for bona fide, professional carriers simply speaks for itself. Some difficulties associated with advanced aging also have some of the characteristics of developmental disability and may or may not be problematic for travel.

Overcoming Barriers

Outside of the United States many, if not most, quality properties are sensitive and conscious of the need to reduce and/or eliminate unnecessary barriers to guest mobility issues. Buildings of more than two stories will typically have elevators, and entrances will often have ramped alternatives to the sometimes "impressive staircase." In much of the world outside of the U.S., however, do not anticipate that every curb will have ramped curb cuts, or that every stair or even every high threshold will have a ramped alternative. Many older buildings dating back to perhaps the Middle Ages tend to be on narrow streets with a high curb or step into the property to allow storm water and/or sewage (at one time) to flow away from the interior of the building. In most parts of the world, it is not possible, or not a priority, to retrofit every historic building to meet Americans with Disabilities Act (ADA) standards. Much of the travel-oriented world, however, has become increasingly sensitive to special needs of some travelers and their own residents as well.

Limits on Accessibility

Many hotels and cruise ships limit the total number of rooms with fully accessible bathtubs, showers, and even accessible doorways. Staterooms aboard a cruise ship may limit accessibility to the interior cabins only, or may have few ideal alternatives in the event that the plumbing stops up in the accessible cabin. A big consideration is the ability to make a transfer from a wheelchair either with or without assistance with respect to taxis, shuttle buses, rental cars, and other modes of transportation. Despite major efforts to be more accommodating, public buses often get overcrowded and require a passenger to either wait for a less full bus, or ride standing up and holding onto the "monkey bars" for the same full fare as the seated passengers. Travelers with luggage may find it extremely difficult to manage bags up and down the aisles as the public bus lurches forward and makes abrupt stops. One solution is to spend a distinct amount more money and take the taxi from curb to curb.

Ramp Accessibility

Boat ramps and docks can be especially difficult for the mobility-impaired traveler. Ramps off major ships may appear to have a reasonable slope at one time and, after changing tides, may be far steeper to ascend or descend at another time. In Alaska the slope of the ramp often varies dramatically from debarkation to embarkation because of the substantial variation between high and low tides. Some ship ramps are limited to stairs only rather than a

143

smooth surface. Also, when a ship must anchor away from the dock, getting into a tender craft can be very difficult due to the tender's bobbing up and down as you step onto it.

Restaurant Accessibility

Restaurants throughout the world have much in common and certainly do value the importance of all potential diners who are capable of paying the bill and of therefore contributing to their business success. The restaurant property with little or no accommodation for special needs will typically lose group sales, not just the occasional lone diner. Some slack, of course, must be given to historic facilities that may well have difficult stairs or other architectural obstructions such as a restroom in the basement or up a flight of stairs that is not amenable to correction. Most newer facilities are quite conscious of the occasional special needs of the public (or building code obligates specific accommodations) that will facilitate their business in the long run. Sometimes, a going establishment is put out of business because it must retrofit with elevators and ramps and other requirements that are simply cost prohibitive for that business. Building codes for new facilities will often include curb cuts to allow access from the street or parking lot to the sidewalk, wide entry doors that are relatively easy to open, and little or no threshold problem. Restaurants are often more sensitive to the need for wider aisles between tables and chairs to allow wheelchair access. There must also be some moveable chairs for the person who will remain in a wheelchair and, more importantly, there is the need for accessible bathrooms with at least one area that is suitable for wheelchair use. Most restaurants are attentive to improving accessibility design and it has become a major benefit for employees and customers alike.

Suggestions for Additional Information

www.disabilitytravel.com
www.disabilityworld.org
www.europeforvisitors.com
www.geocities.com
www.independentliving.org.
www.transitionsabroad.com

18
Safe Travel

To climb steep hills requires slow pace
at first.—William Shakespeare

Your Passport to Adventure

For general safety in any foreign country it is prudent to anticipate that some official may ask to see your passport. A flimsy excuse that you cannot seem to find your passport might lead to your detention until the identification issue is resolved. Be especially diligent about protecting your passport and other government-issued identification. In a separate place keep back-up copies of all relevant IDs. In case of loss or possible theft, you will have relevant passport numbers, expiration dates, and additional documentation to verify who you are. The same suggestion applies to credit cards that may need to be suddenly cancelled, or a medical card accessed. Recently, a cruise passenger visiting St. Petersburg, Russia, told this writer at dinner that he had accidentally lost his passport between the bedspread and the headboard of his cabin.

He worried about exiting the country and nearly had to pay very substantial replacement fees, but the passport was found by the housekeeping staff and the crisis passed without further incident.

Sensitivity to Local Laws

Organized tours or excursions with respected, experienced, and well-financed tour operators will almost always be guiding tourists within the local laws and customs that are both interesting and safe. It is the tourist who intentionally gets away from the tour guides and who pushes the limits to do something chancy on his/her own who may increase the risk of violating a local law. In Mexico, for example, this writer observed a young U.S. Coast Guard man returning from a snorkel trip to a small island with an iguana lizard on a small leash. He had traded his watch for the "pet." We later heard that he had been held overnight in jail for violating the endangered species law. His release was costly and, of course, he lost both his watch and the iguana. In Tiananmen Square of Beijing, China, a tour guide told us that if it felt like our group of travelers were being too tightly surrounded by vendors, to loudly shout, "Police!" The unlicensed vendors, who sometimes get overzealous, will typically disperse.

Sensitivity to Marginal or Unfamiliar Areas

Leisure travelers can typically identify marginal areas that do not appear receptive to the needs and interests of visitors. The absence of street and storefront vendors, public eating establishments, and public restrooms are potential indicators. An area can appear quite impoverished yet be quite safe, but the presence of too much debris and poor water and sewage systems could be a health hazard and, late at night, not a safe place to be. Physical assaults on travelers from any nation are rare in most parts of the world except for those persons who appear to be overly reckless about their personal safety.

Safety often begins with careful observation of your surroundings. An imperfection in a walking area can be a minor annoyance or actually lead to a fall with a serious injury. Not every possible safety hazard of travel comes with a posted warning sign. In urban areas it is especially important to make personal safety observations as crowds grow bigger and as the evening becomes later and later. At such times, in virtually every city around the world, there are increased risks for travelers who loiter in marginal, unfamiliar areas. The value of international tourism is such, however, that any incident that receives widespread media attention is something that local governments and business people alike want very much to avoid. One solution is to carefully follow your tour guide's advice. Another option is to ask a hotel concierge or hotel manager about areas that are safe or that should be avoided.

Conceal Your Financial Assets

For an extra level of financial safety, conceal cash and credit cards within different parts of your clothing so you will never be caught without funds to make phone calls, or pay a taxi, or pay a charge that you have just made. Options include keeping some back-up cash inside a sock, a shoe, inside a money belt or neck pouch, a hat, a jacket, or a secret compartment in a piece of luggage. Each person can do the same to spread out possible risk factors. Another option is to pre-arrange to have someone wire money to you in the case of an emergency. The general rule of travel is that you tend to spend somewhat more money than you anticipated. The important factor is to budget for the unexpected and to allow for a financial cushion in case of something like an emergency expense. A valid credit card can be a good back-up for such payments. An American Express card without tight credit limits can also be a good travel asset for dealing with the unexpected. Another suggested precaution is to make arrangements to have your personal photograph placed on your credit card.

Use Your Own Good Judgment

Swimming and wading pools used by travelers typically have a sign posted that says "No Lifeguard On Duty." Such notices make it increasingly apparent that it is the parent's or guardian's responsibility to constantly observe the personal safety of small children around water, or any potential hazard, to ensure that the child does not have a problem. Also, if you purchase a large and/ or heavy object as you travel, you may have to carry that object yourself all the way back home.

Conceal Minor Frustrations with Politeness

Being polite, courteous, and attentive to others will produce better results than rudeness. In some instances, there may be a few people along the way who are rude, caustic, or antagonistic in some way. The real goal is to avoid escalating a small, isolated event into a confrontation, and to make the best of the situation, move on, and continue to have a great vacation experience. To most of the world's people it is the American or the Canadian who is the foreigner, not the other way around. Your potential to be a representative for peaceful international exchange is very real.

Additional Information Suggestions

www.baby-everywhere.com
www.corporatetravelsafety.com
www.ecology.org
www.kidsource.com
www.navigant.com
www.parenthood.com
www.safecanada.ca

www.safewithin.com
www.smarttravel.gov
www.smarttravel.org
www.travelsafe.com
www.travelsafely.com
www.travmed.com
www.womentraveltips.com

19
Travel Hazards

Like all great travelers, I have seen more than I remember, and remember more than I have seen. —Benjamin Disraeli

Crossing the Street Has Risks

Everything in life has some degree of risk associated with it. Crossing the street or going down stairs is a calculated risk yet we do it all of the time. A British study concluded that on a per-mile basis commercial airline transportation was actually safer than walking. A more serious travel hazard that is commonly found is simply shopping too much. Another hazard is the periodic annoyance that results from unpredictability of the weather. In the event of a fairly sudden hurricane in the Caribbean, for instance, a cruise ship will re-route to safer destinations and move out of harm's way based on top-quality, satellite-GPS navigation systems and visual-satellite plotting of exactly what the hurricane is doing. Travelers at a fixed destination such as New Orleans, Cancun, Cayman Islands, and others who find themselves in a storm's path must "weather out" the consequences of the storm with little alternative except to batten down the shutters, cover big windows with plywood, load up the car, and evacuate the threatened area. Recently, major distinctions were found by some travelers booking through the Internet giants, such as Travelocity, Expedia.com, and Orbitz compared to booking through their personal travel agent. Storm victims who left their documents behind were typically unable to gain relocation assistance from the Internet giants. Travelers in the same situation who had a personal travel agent were able to call, speak to the person who booked them, and typically receive relocation assistance whether they had documents in their possession or not.

No Insurance, No Recourse

Traveling without insurance can be one of the greatest possible hazards. Imagine being a perfectly healthy adult on a cruise and suddenly having a serious fall somewhere along the route, or an unexpected medical problem that absolutely requires more than a couple of aspirin or a few bandages. The cruise ship medical staff may insist that you be air-lifted to the nearest appropriate medical facility. The cost of such air rescue, without insurance coverage, could make a very substantial impact on your vacation budget for years to come. There is also the potential that there could be language barriers between patient and medical staff. This could be especially true of land vacations to remote areas. Another possibility is not having cancellation insurance and then learning that there has been an extreme emergency or death in the family just before you were scheduled to depart. Cancellation at certain points without insurance could cost you the unused tour or cruise price. See www.travelguard.com for additional details.

Some travelers try to "save" on the initial expense of travel by skipping on travel insurance. Occasionally, however, a vendor bankruptcy may be near. The insurance underwriters may not know about an impending bankruptcy until it is officially declared. If the travel insurer will not insure a particular travel package, ask the reason. You could lose whatever you paid if the travel vendor goes out of business prior to the start of your vacation. Many insurers do not cover the major airlines that are in bankruptcy. Solution: Carefully look at the reasons for and value in buying travel insurance before rejecting the idea just to "save on travel expenses."

An Injury Can Suddenly Spoil a Vacation
Avoid unusually risky sports activity that could lead to a very confining injury or need to be treated in an unfamiliar clinic or hospital. Many destinations around the world do not have the same safety standards as the U.S. Absence of handrails, poorly maintained stairs, and uneven streets can increase the risk of an injurious fall. There is an old expression, or perhaps an old joke, that says you should travel because most injuries occur in the home. Actually, there is some merit to warnings that accidents often occur while doing everyday tasks and not giving prevention a great deal of thought. The American Academy of Orthopedic Surgeons recently indicated that up to 60% of fall injuries occur in the patient's home and are usually a part of everyday activities. Up to 30% of accidental falls occur in public places. The remaining 10% of fall injuries, especially for patients in the age 65+ range, occur in hospitals, retirement facilities, nursing homes, and related institutions. Being observant and cautious in new settings may be a very basic recommendation but is still among the best preventatives for avoiding an injury that could disrupt a vacation.

Why Buy Travel Insurance?
One company, Travel Guard International, provides travel insurance for more than 6 million travelers worldwide each year. The value (peace of mind) received is the primary reason that the insurance is purchased in the first place. Travel insurance includes trip cancellation, travel interruption, delays, emergency medical expenses, lost baggage, emergency medical evacuation, and 24-hour assistance service. For a very reasonable cost, you can protect your travel investment and your health needs in case of a medical emergency. To verify coverage for yourself, call your medical insurance provider and ask if you are covered and if so, is the

coverage primary or secondary medical care outside of the United States? Ask if they will wire money to a foreign medical facility in advance (not after-the-fact) to provide the care you may need at the moment you need it. Most travel insurance companies offer a variety of different levels of coverage. Some offer both primary and secondary coverage. Your travel consultant should be able to help you with making a decision on which policy to purchase.

Insurance Suppliers and Resources to Consider:
- Access America www.accessamerica.com
- Global Alert www.totaltravelinsurance.com
- Center for Disease Control www.cdc.gov/travel
- CSA Travel Protection www.csatravelprotection.com
- Travel Guard International www.travelguard.com
- Travel Insured www.travelinsured.com

For air evacuation information in advance consider:
- AirMed International 800-356-2161
- International Society of Travel Medicine www.istm.org
- Medjet Assist www.medjetassist.com

Observe Local Laws

The chance of being arrested while doing typical tourist activity may be very slight but may become a reality in a very unfamiliar area such as driving a rental car on the opposite side of the street or after too much local food and drink. Other countries have their own laws. If millions of tourists journey to a particular destination without incident, one over-dramatized event should not be used to penalize all of the investors and service providers who risk so much to make travelers feel welcome, safe, and comfortable. Ideally, all news reports would be first placed in context, but that obviously would not sell as many newspapers, or attract as many TV viewers. As a world traveler, you can match any isolated incident against the millions of people who conduct their lives without incident.

Air Sickness

A known medical condition for some people should be discussed with your doctor or maybe a trusted pharmacist before planning a flight. There may be a suitable medication that will be helpful. For most people this seems to be a very rare condition aboard commercial airliners with pressurized cabins and typically fairly smooth and efficient service compared to traveling the same miles by other means. Persons who are prone to either extreme air sickness or sea sickness are encouraged to seek medical assistance. For some very special people it may make more sense to consider vicarious travel in the great world of books and film.

Potentially Tainted Food

Each part of the world has some indigenous bacteria, virus, or chemical variations in water systems, food products, and food handling that may have some impact on your dietary comfort level and sense of well being. Four- or five-star dining facilities throughout the world will not likely be a problem, or perhaps a minor inconvenience that soon goes away. The big risk factors are likely to be found with street vendors who lack all sign of sanitation facilities, refrigeration, and even keeping the flies off. Among the big risks for eating "fun, fast food" from a street vendor in a foreign area is that the tainted food could become a source of salmonella poisoning and directly cause serious illness. For extra precautions, consider drinking only from bottled liquids, carrying your own hand-packed snacks, and using hand-cleaning soaps or chemicals before eating.

Overeating

A common discomfort on a vacation where there seems to be an abundance of buffet-style dining opportunities is the potential to load the plate with so many different flavors, and calories, that you are left with unpleasant memories, and maybe extra pounds that you were not expecting. It is not uncommon for many restaurants to serve overly large portions to create a positive image and to encourage longer dining times that may include more alcohol sales to help boost their revenue. Meals served in multiple courses also tend to increase the potential for distinct overeating. Various options include minimizing the trips to the buffet, or cutting way back on seriously sampling everything that looks good. Focus more on the fruits and vegetables that tend to be very healthy but rather tedious to prepare in such quantities and varieties at home. And seriously cut back on high-fat and high-sugar foods that are cooked in oils of one kind or another.

Pre-existing Conditions

Special diets, such as diabetic diets, or low-sodium, low-sugar diets, or any anti-allergy diet require special attention to be sure the food preparation meets your particular needs. Asking the food server how something was prepared may be a high-risk method and produce very unreliable results, especially if there are language barriers. The international traveler at all ages will benefit from a careful review of travel health insurance before departure. When you purchase travel insurance to cover pre-existing conditions, you must follow precise guidelines at the time of purchase relative to the first payment for the travel package.

Additional Information Sources

www.cdc.gov/travel
www.dangerousdestinations.com
www.emoryhealthcare.org
www.flidgrp.com/hazards.shtml
www.foodsmart.com.au/hazards
www.joetourist.ca/traveltips
www.ncbi.nlm.nih.gov
www.traveldoctor.co.uk/accidents
www.travelguard.com
www.wellness.colostate.edu/travel

20
Health Concerns

It is good to have an end to journey toward; but it is the journey that matters in the end. —Ursula Le Guin

Carry Bottled Water

Just a few decades ago very few people would have willingly paid for bottled water. A traveler would have typically carried a thermos of either hot or cold liquid, or filled a glass from the nearest water faucet. Now, caution about water quality has spawned billion-dollar industries selling filtered water throughout the world. The sale of bottled water has become so pervasive in many places that when you request water at a restaurant you will typically be offered the choice of bottled water (for sale, of course), or a glass of water. It is common now to carry bottled water to avoid exposure to unfamiliar microbes in distant locales. Bottled water can also be used to wash hands periodically and bottled drinks can be an alternative to possibly tainted ice cubes.

Avoid Dehydration

Air transportation has unique issues related to dehydration because of close proximities for extended periods and breathing recycled air at very high altitudes. Suggestions for improving the experience include regular drinking of water and juices and minimizing or postponing dehydrating drinks such as alcohol and caffeinated drinks. Lining your nose with a mild anti-bacterial cream may assist. A supply of handiwipes is good along with washing with soap and water. Air filter products that can be worn around the neck can possibly assist with viral infections. A severe cold or flu is not a pleasant way to begin or end a vacation.

Special Medications

Prescription medications require special planning. Order sufficient amounts of prescription medications in advance. Pack enough of the needed medications in your carry-on baggage. Let

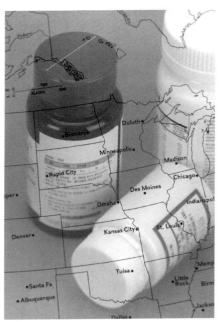

your doctor and/or pharmacist know where you are going so medications can be labeled in ways that are likely to be understood by inspectors or pharmacists at the new destination. Ask your travel consultant to check on the rules (laws) regarding travel with your medications in the different countries on your itinerary. Very large amounts of medication can give a wrong impression when luggage is inspected. Translations from one language to another can also be strange. Example: Fighting a small cold, this writer visited a quaint German town as part of a Rhine-Main-Danube river cruise and stopped at a pharmacy to buy cough drops (lozenges). The pharmacist, naturally enough, offered a bottle of liquid cough "drops" to be applied to the throat with a dropper. After some verbal wrangling, the pharmacist did offer lozenges, which she considered quite inferior to the liquid drops. Travelers who carry prescription drugs, however, should keep them in the original prescription containers and possibly have a letter from the prescribing physician that describes the need to have the drugs. Such a letter can be especially important for diabetics who carry needles and syringes, or anyone carrying narcotic drugs.

Confirm Special Needs in Advance

For wheelchairs, walkers, or other medical appliances, advance confirmation may be needed for boarding and deboarding planes, ships, trains, cars, buses, and shuttles. ADA rules within the United States usually do not apply in other destinations. Accessibility can be a minor or major issue in the absence of good elevators and other provisions to assist the mobility-impaired. A stopped-up toilet in an accessible room or cabin can be most awkward if the nearest available facility has very limited accessibility. Old cities in Europe and Asia often have areas with narrow, bumpy, and steep walkways or roads that may not be recommended for wheelchair travel. Power wheelchairs can also create different issues if they cannot be collapsed, or cannot get over high thresholds such as on many ships.

Watch the Water System

In some areas of the world, it is important to brush your teeth with bottled water because the local water is unsafe for travelers to drink. For the same reasons it can be helpful to avoid getting shower water in your eyes or mouth. If in doubt about the water system, drink only bottled liquids and avoid ice cubes. When it is convenient, you can boil water that you intend to drink or to use for cooking. Water should boil at a good rolling rate for at least 10 minutes for purification. Letting the water cool slowly also allows possible sedimentation to go to the bottom and to remain there if poured off carefully. In Puerto Vallarta, for instance, there is a city-wide water purification system and the water is safe to drink from the tap. That is not necessarily true of all cities in Mexico or many other parts of the world. Recently I stayed at the St. Regis Hotel in Shanghai, China, a five-star property with every amenity one could imagine. However, there were several complimentary bottles of water in the room that were placed in strategic locations such as on the night stands and by the sink in the bathroom. The implied message was that one should brush his/her teeth with the bottled water and not drink from the tap.

A Floating Resort, Not a Bobbing Cork

Cruise ships take full advantage of their enormous size, special stabilizers, and detailed weather reports to avoid severe weather conditions when possible, and re-route as necessary. Unlike a resort hotel that may be in the path of a hurricane, a cruise ship simply moves out of its path. Fortunately, most people do not suffer from nausea or sea-sickness. But for those who do have motion sensitivity, there are preventative medications such as Dramamine, behind-the-ear medications such as Motion Eaze, and pressure-point wristbands that can be helpful. Basic precautions can also include avoidance of spicy or unfamiliar foods, overindulgence at the buffet, and too much alcohol.

Little Accessories Can Be a Big Help

Carry the simple little extras that can be hard to find in a strange or new location. Small plastic bags, for instance, can have many different uses. Carry a few bandages, ointment, lotion, handiwipes, maybe an ace bandage in case of a slight sprain, sun block, sun glasses, a simple hat to keep rain and sun off as desired, and a plastic raincoat that folds up to the size of a man's wallet.

No Cash, No Credit, No Insurance, No Treatment

Many foreign hospitals and clinics require that money be paid in advance before they will proceed with treatment and not all health insurance companies will wire money to a foreign destination. Be sure to validate the differences between primary and secondary insurance requirements before you go. Also, be certain to inform your credit card company(s) that you will be in particular areas at particular times and not at your usual residence so the pre-programmed computer does not cut you off at a very awkward time. It can also be helpful to carry a credit card from a different company and ideally without harsh upper limits such as American Express.

158

Insurance Suppliers and Resources to Consider:
- Access America www.accessamerica.com
- Global Alert www.totaltravelinsurance.com
- Center for Disease Control www.cdc.gov/travel
- CSA Travel Protection www.csatravelprotection.com
- Travel Guard International www.travelguard.com
- Travel Insured www.travelinsured.com

For air evacuation information in advance consider:
- AirMed International 800-356-2161
- International Society of Travel Medicine www.istm.org
- Medjet Assist www.medjetassist.com

Cleanliness Varies

Observe the local food handlers carefully. Do the grocers and food vendors use plastic gloves for handling food, or just handle food and much-less-than-sanitary currency without any sign of washing up? A major side effect of diarrhea, besides discomfort, is dehydration. Take special steps to re-hydrate with recommended liquids that have some actual sugar content, not just bottled water that is supposedly completely sterile. Typically a good travel idea is to carry a small first aid kit of your own making that can be very helpful for the little knicks, scrapes, and cuts that occur in the natural progress of a day, yet could quickly turn into a difficult infection if ignored. Small packages of antibacterial moist wipes are typically easy to carry and can be very helpful when soap and clean water are not readily available. Adhesive moleskin can likewise be helpful to minimize possible blisters.

Stay Healthy, Be Happy

In general, avoid places where there may be a concentration of illness or signs of poor sanitation. Use lots of hand soap on a regular basis and even carry a small bar of soap for those situations where it appears to be lacking. Ordinary soap, when used thoroughly, has been shown to be just as effective as "anti-bacterial soaps." Be extra conscious of what you touch with your hands, such as handrails, doorknobs, vendor products, countertops, chairs, and tables, and then touching your eyes, nose, or mouth without using something like sanitary handiwipes.

Medical Records

It is essential to carry at least one copy of your medical identification card and at the very least the full name and contact numbers for the physician who knows you best and who has your current medical records. Foreign hospital staffs, with possibly limited English language skills, might have to call and get your blood type, allergies, and other specific information in the case of an emergency. This is another situation where travel insurance can be very valuable. The insurance providers often have a 24/7 medical assistance line with interpreters. It is also recommended that you consider an identification bracelet if appropriate to acknowledge diabetes, heart condition, pacemaker, or other information that would be essential if you were somehow unable to communicate in an emergency situation.

Additional Sources of Information

www.cdc.gov/travel
www.familydoctor.org
www.mdtravelhealth.com
www.thehtd.org
www.thirdworldtraveler.com

www.traveldoctor.co.uk
www.travelhealthhelp.com
www.tripprep.com
www.vaccinations.com

21
Scams to Avoid

*All that is gold does not glitter, not all those
who wander are lost.* — J.R.R. Tolkien

Generic Disclaimer

A major list of potentially dishonest dealings from potentially isolated cases around the world is not intended to scare travelers who are considering an unfamiliar destination. The purpose in recounting examples of scam behavior is to assist travelers in recognizing some of the possible danger signals. Being forewarned about deceptive behaviors is a way to be more observant and reduces the likelihood of being exploited. The chances are good that none of the situations described below will actually happen to you. However, increasing sensitivity to unfortunate events that might occur is the best preventative to avoid being a victim and to instead be a very happy traveler.

Greed is the Seed of the Scam

Being forewarned is a major step toward avoiding dirty rotten tricks and petty crimes that are not just limited to careless travelers. Take precautions and watch for certain signs – be sensitive to your personal space if you feel you are being crowded. In an unfamiliar setting, keep a buffer of space around you and you can likely travel without being a major victim of theft. Travel reminder: Everyone loves a bargain. The rare find, the unique travel experience, the exciting story to tell when you return are all part of the mystic travel lore that can be told again and again, and may be embellished for the pure joy of it. However, travel scams, cons, and rip-offs can also be a part of some travel experiences (reported or not) and are actually among the most frequent complaints to the Federal Trade Commission (FTC). Scams are typically rare for discriminating travelers but can be a real source of anxiety or financial pain if they do occur. Solution: Precaution and awareness are probably the best things you can do to protect yourself and still have a great travel experience.

Good for Whom?

Enticing offers are sometimes covers for grossly over-priced time shares, an over-hyped vacation package, or resort hotel offer that may have substandard products or services that are costly or even impossible to upgrade to an acceptable level. When we suddenly think we are getting something exceptional at a price that is way below the market, there is a real tendency to not ask probing questions. If we did, maybe the outcome would be very different. Sellers have the opportunity to practice their craft daily and know that within minutes travelers will probably never be seen again. The prospect of outwitting an intentionally shady vendor under such circumstances is not likely. Solution: The traveler's goal is to have a great time and be enriched by new experiences and guard against any big losses, not to worry about a few dollars here and a few dollars there with every transaction that comes along.

The Hook (Teaser)

Most teaser offers are specifically intended to get your attention. The offer itself will be misrepresented, or "sold out." The real purpose is to substantially up-sell or cross-sell you once an interest is expressed. Legitimate 5-star properties simply do not offer 2-star rates and remain in business with top-quality service and reliability. One common rule of thumb for deep, deep discounts is that when cost must be cut, it is the service that is the first to go. Next to go is product and vendor reliability. You can forget all about refunds, service warranties, and guarantees when you do business with substandard vendors. The long-standing, general rule of thumb is, "If it sounds too good to be true, it usually is." Solution: Validate all teaser claims, or just ignore them.

The Numbers Racket

Outdoor ATM machines are especially vulnerable to telescopic or zoom lenses that may be trained on the keypad of an unsuspecting user. So-called "memory experts" can observe and memorize your pin number for future reference. Later, the trick is to gain access to your bank card by one stealthy means or another to go back and make major hits upon your account. One solution is to use travel ATMs as infrequently as possible and then try to limit usage to the interior of quality hotels or banks and place the other hand or some visual obstruction over the key pad as pin numbers are being input. Another reason for picking ATM sites carefully is to avoid the "sticking card scam" where you may have to leave your card in the machine because no one is available to assist in extracting the card, or if someone suddenly appears to offer "help."

"You've Been Randomly Selected"

Unsolicited phone calls, mailers, fax, or e-mails that say, "You've just won a vacation," should be either ignored, or verified. If you cannot verify details to your satisfaction, contact the source by external means and also get the full names of the people that you contacted. Beware of telemarketers with big promises and little or no documentation that can be verified. Also, be leery of travel clubs that charge big, up-front fees for membership (they can go bankrupt and leave you with only a bad memory of the experience). Consider the Federal Trade Commission, attorney general's office of your state, and even Internet cross-referencing if there is the slightest doubt about the source. You might call the resort or airline directly to confirm details. Offers of something being free are often disguises for hidden costs, or non-existent services. Many such offers are specifically intended to exploit the good intentions of distinctly elderly individuals. Solution: Ask for a phone number to call that person right back. Rarely, if ever, will you get the caller's number. The simple alternative is to hang up the phone, or slow them down by asking if you can put them on hold for a moment and go back to whatever you were doing before being so rudely interrupted.

"You're the Lucky Winner"

Only the most gullible people believe in winning luxury travel vacations at random, or due to some drawing that's really intended to get your name, address, and contact information for future sales contacts. Careful verification will almost always expose these offers as phonies. Do not be a victim. Bitter memories last a long time when it takes months and months to recover a portion, if any, of the dollars you too quickly paid to a fraudulent source. Beware of winning a "travel prize," a "sweepstakes," a "drawing," or similar windfall. This is especially true for unexpected telephone calls that build up your excitement and expect a commitment, such as your credit card number, during the same call. Telephone guarantees that deposits are fully refundable should be considered worthless until all verifications are complete, and requests for shipping cost payment in advance should never be paid.

Evaluate Your Travel Consultant's Credentials

Reputable consultants are proud of their professional affiliations, training, experience, insurance coverage, and licensing (where required). Additional credentials can include a posted bond, errors and omissions insurance, and study of travel publications that report on both positive and negative aspects of the travel business. Also, a well-qualified travel consultant has a business address that can all be verified, not just a business card. Wise travelers will be leery of the once-in-awhile "travel agent" who merely forwards you on to someone else and asks you to present their pin number to begin the process of booking a vacation. For obvious reasons, such agents are often described as "pin number agents," or "card mill agents," who have little or no travel training and likely do not have any professional affiliations, errors and omissions insurance, or a good reputation with travel wholesalers. Most travel consultants have taken the time to educate themselves on specific destinations and have become Destination Specialists (e.g., Mexico, Hawaii, Switzerland, etc.). Others are cruise or tour specialists. It pays to ask about a travel consultant's credentials such as CTC (Certified Travel Consultant), MCC (Master Cruise Counsellor), ECC (Elite Cruise Counsellor), etc.

Verify What You Are Getting

Verify the cancellation procedures even with trusted vendors and agents. The minority of bogus sources typically use delaying tactics and finally disappear—with your money. Watch for offer omissions such as the following: no meals, no taxes, no tips, no deposits, no surcharges, no upgrades, no view, no refunds, or must join a club to qualify for indicated benefits. Be extremely cautious about giving out credit card information except to verifiable sources. Watch for ads that give few details yet promise lots of excitement for very little money. Be cautious of any source that asks for money before confirming reservations, gathering and sharing all necessary information, and before explaining the written cancellation and refund procedures. Solution: Watch surprise situations where decisions must be made immediately. Slow down the process and use the time to verify the facts.

Exchanging Currency

Use official currency exchange facilities for situations where credit cards cannot be used. Many banks tend to discourage international money exchange because of low profits and the long lines that often result. One source of currency conversion information is www.xe.com/ucc. For holidays and possible closures in foreign destinations consider www.bank-holidays.com. Smaller retailers tend to give themselves the benefit of any doubt regarding exchange rates, and will typically make change in the local currency. If you change too much cash to the foreign currency, it can cost you again to convert back when you get home. The obvious solution is to use your credit card wherever possible at hotels, restaurants, large retailers, and tour companies or rental agencies. Solution:

Your credit card company does the exchange rate conversion for you and at the best terms at the moment of conversion. Most credit card companies will charge a small conversion fee. Check with your credit card company before departing on your trip.

Where Pickings Are Good

Pickpockets can be anywhere and even young children may be working as a team. Be especially careful about taking out money and revealing where you keep it. A second or third "fake" wallet is a good strategy for carrying one-dollar bills for tipping and small purchases. Keep that wallet where you normally keep "the real wallet." Possibly keep large rubber bands around the real wallet and keep it in a secure place. Credit card, passport, and other (government issued) photo identification should be kept in other secure places (inside a sock can be good). Never flash a big bank roll or display whatever might be taken for "wealth." Avoid money clips and identification holders with neck straps that could lead to yanking injuries. Keep good duplicates of ID, passport, and credit cards in case of emergency and in secure places such as hotel or cabin safe. Consider double-lined fanny packs and keep the pack concealed by wearing it under a loose jacket or shirt. Pickpockets use razor knives to slice open fanny packs or strap bags in ways you will probably never feel. It is literally amazing to observe re-enactments of how easily wristwatches and necklaces can be removed without the victim noticing. In an electronic world the big money is in stealing identifications that can be quickly exploited for big returns, little risk, plus lasting pain and embarrassment for the victim. Pickpockets and scammers *are never* social workers with a heart. For them, it is just a job. Solution: Guard your personal space, consider a decoy wallet, use something like a money belt for critical ID, and use credit cards that have your photograph.

The Innocent Conversation

Airport shuttle buses can be fertile areas for major crime. The shuttle passenger with "friendly" questions about where you're going, whether someone is watching your house, or if you have a house alarm, may seem innocent enough until they're able to steal your address by devious methods, and break in while you are away. Another ploy is for one accomplice in the shuttle bus to quickly get off behind the driver. The other accomplice stages a distraction, such as a fall in the aisle or going down the steps to the curb that blocks the exit for a few precious seconds, and the first accomplice claims a bag of choice and quickly exits with it. Solution: Avoid giving out accurate information about your vacation plans except to those who really need to know. Keep track of your luggage (especially if there is a distraction).

The Metal Detector Ploy

Like the shuttle bus ploy, a person in front of you at the airport screening gate sets off the alarm and then blocks your passage while an accomplice grabs whatever you placed on the conveyor and disappears. Let the person ahead of you clear the metal detector before placing your personal items on the conveyor. It can get very confusing all of a sudden when you have placed valuables on the conveyor for screening and you are asked to stand aside and be screened by a hand-held wand. Unless you are traveling alone, possibly rehearse how you will look after each other's carry-on items and pocket or purse contents. Solution: Let the person ahead of you fully clear the metal detector before you step through.

The Camera Ploy

A willing volunteer, or even an apparent vendor with a pet animal, offers to take a couple's photo and then demands cash for the photo, or to return the camera, or runs off with the camera. Solution: Carry a disposable camera for the few shots of yourselves together. Most scam artists know enough to "go for the good stuff" when they do risk injury or arrest that rarely happens to them. Solution: Preserve the high-quality digital camera for your own shots only.

General Rule Number One

Do not wear expensive or even expensive-looking jewelry while touring impoverished or crowded urban areas. Expensive-appearing jewelry may target you as a likely victim. Regrettably, precious jewelry that is packed in checked (and x-rayed!) airline luggage has been known to disappear without a trace. Solution: Keep travel jewelry simple and carry it on your person.

General Rule Number Two

Avoid purchasing and using any health products that are grossly discounted and especially if sold by street vendors. Fake perfumes, for instance, lack the expensive binders that hold the pleasant aroma and may cause severe allergic reactions. The wrong sunglasses can actually lead to eye injury. Sun screen without actual blockers could lead to severe burns. Anything taken internally can have unpredictable consequences if not produced by legal, ethical sources that are accountable for any injuries that may result. Unsafe or unsanitary products, at any price, can quickly spoil a vacation. Solution: Do not buy health or cosmetic products from street vendors.

Keep Some Elbow Room

Simple precautions against scams and thefts include being sensitive to your personal space. Be especially wary and reposition yourself if you sense one or more persons are suddenly intruding on your space. Be observant of people wearing loose garments that can quickly conceal a snatched item, especially if the weather is hot. Do not assume that someone is honest because he/she has the appearance of a "clean-cut college kid." Do not hang purses on the inside door hook of public lavatories. A crook can reach over, grab the purse, and vanish. With strapped purses, bags, and luggage with straps, try to keep them within an easy field of vision and if set down, actually stand on the strap and avoid being jostled by anyone who gets near you. Pickpockets must know which pocket to pick (and they read you very well in advance). Consider a decoy pocketbook to spread out the risk. Keep lots of tip money and small denomination bills in one place and precious identification cards, credit cards, and large denomination bills in another place, such as undergarment document/money holders. Solution: Be conscious of suddenly "being crowded" by local residents who seem to be overly familiar.

Distract, Grab, and Run

Hot, sunny beaches are favored "work sites" for scam artists who typically work in pairs or larger groupings. The goal is to sight someone who has left his/her bag to go into the water, or is just catching sun without seeing exactly where the beach bag is located. One person creates a diversion (claims of something out in the water, a fake fight, etc.) and the accomplice casually walks off with the beach bag. Free drinks may be offered at the beach or beside the swimming pool with a request to see or take the hotel key card and room number to verify that you are a guest of that property. Within minutes someone can gain access to your room and grab valuable contents that you thought, a moment ago, were secure. Solution: Consider a high-quality swimsuit with secure inside pockets for identification, credit, and room or car keys. Consider the water-tight containers for cash, identification, or keys that can be worn under a swimsuit. A simple solution is to keep one-dollar bills tucked away for those little purchases, not big bills.

"What Would You Give Me For …?"

Watch for gold watch and gold necklace scams. The appearance is that you may be saving very large amounts of money, or maybe living on the edge a bit and buying a hot item that a desperate seller is willing to sell for pennies on the dollar. The reality is that the objects being sold cost the vendor pennies, not dollars and anything they can get from the unwary tourist tends to be profit to them. This writer was once offered a chance to buy five "Rolex" watches for $10.00 from a street vendor while standing with a tour group in Shanghai, China. The watches, of course, are simple imitations and tend to be called "looky looky" watches because the hands sometimes fall off when you turn them over. Solution: Assume you are buying novelty junk, or just say no.

Feature Movies "Almost Free"

The blank video scam is pretty amazing. Willing tourists, especially those influenced by their children, are encouraged to buy "pirated" first-run films for something like $10 each or two for $15.00. The two-hour films of in-demand movies are typically

169

either blank, or maybe have only fifteen minutes of video tape. In other cases the actual images and sound quality may be very substandard. The illusion created in the buyer's mind is that the purchase was a rare bargain. Solution: First-run, copyrighted material does not sell for ten cents on the dollar.

Buy a Piece of Paradise and Never Stop Paying

Carefully research the subject of time shares well in advance of travel if you think you might be a candidate for this type of vacation plan. Verify for yourself that most U.S. banks will not provide financing and the reasons that banks will not finance. That information should tell you much about the issues you should consider in making a decision to purchase or not. Also, consider contacting local sources that are trying to re-sell existing time-share that the present owners no longer want. Verify how much the owner's cost can increase in the case of a hurricane or other types of damage, not just the initial cost of the time-share. Try to verify all of the details and not rely on a glossy romantic brochure image. Reminder: Non-time-share resorts with major investments to protect often will not allow time-share sales people to do business on their property.

Time-Share Teasers

In some of the world's destinations, time-share promoters can be spotted along sidewalks wherever travelers are likely to congregate. There may be a real temptation to accept a free meal and offers of cash to attend a time-share presentation for a few hours. The street salespeople tend to single out tourists who appear to have the financial means to buy an interest in a condominium property. If you go, others at the presentation will use vacation-time-consuming persuasion techniques to convince you that you are acquiring "an investment" in resort features at a bargain price. The worst example seen recently just outside of a 5-star resort property in Mexico was a fellow that this writer thought was part of the resort's hospitality staff. Instead, it was the typical offer and typical disclaimer that "all you have to do is play the game and then just say no." This aggressive salesperson promised a free meal, free ride to the property, and $200 in cash for attending a 90-minute presentation, but only after he received a $30 USD "refundable" deposit. It didn't take much effort to get him to drop the ridiculous "refundable deposit" and no assurances were made about keeping the appointment to be picked up the next day.

The typical *modus operandi* is for the van to pick up the tourists who thought they would "play the game" of getting something for nothing and drive them way out to a partially developed property or one in the process of "major renovations," and, after a meal, start in with one presentation after another of all of the great features and the "enormous advantages" of owning a time share. There tends to be tremendous pressure to make a same day decision to buy direct from the developer. As the day wears on you may find there are great delays in getting the anticipated transportation back, or you have to figure out a way to get a taxi on your own. The chance of getting any of the cash promised (maybe in pesos and not dollars) is extraordinarily difficult and then only if you pass through a number of additional closing sessions that appear to be right out of *The Godfather* by Mario Puzo.

Few hard facts are disclosed about the total, true costs of a time share. Besides the acquisition cost there are maintenance costs, management costs, taxes, insurance, and maybe special assessments for any number of reasons. The total costs can be a nightmare and the prospect of returning to the same, sometimes overrated property for one to two weeks a year for years to come is very discouraging for some and okay for others. The trick is to know what you are doing. Research all of the possible review sources and financial lending sources you can before allowing yourself to get caught up in the "something for nothing" promises that you may seriously regret later. Many people purchase time shares and are happy with their choice.

It is no secret that up to 50% of the time-share developer's costs are for marketing. The really tawdry image of poorly upgraded hotels as time shares is now mostly gone. Some of the world's biggest developers, such as Marriott and Disney, are also in the business and a majority of properties are as outstanding as they are high priced. Too often time shares are over-sold at inflated, developer's prices to "happy-go-lucky travelers" as an investment. Elizabeth Razzi of *Kiplinger's Personal Finance Magazine* (2001) describes time shares as "a lousy investment." However, whether you agree or not depends mostly on how close you live to the time share and whether you are financially strong or weak.

As a time-share user, you must consider transportation cost as part of the cost of going back to the same property every year. A time-share trader can use points to go to different properties but still has transportation cost as a minimum, and may have to pass on other great vacations such as a cruise, a tour, or many other more flexible options. But if you are going to buy a time-share, consider the resale market and the foreclosure market first. You can save up to approximately 50% and learn a great deal about what you really need to know to be a "happy time-share owner." Then, if you never get behind on payments, you may have something that can at least be called an investment after roughly five to ten years. Solution: Do your own extensive research in advance, not at the free breakfast.

Additional Sources of Information

www.bet.com/travel/howtoavoidatravelscam.htm
www.corporatetravelsafety.com
www.crimes-of-persuasion.com
www.fact-sheets.com/travel
www.fraud.org/tips/internet/travelfraud.htm
www.ftc.gov
www.healthandage.com
www.hotelmarketing.com
www.msnbc.msn.com
www.smartertravel.com
www.tanserve.com/towns/scams.html
www.travelsense.org

22
Security

Travel is the frivolous part of serious lives, and the serious part of frivolous ones. —Anne Sophie Swetchine

Travel Insurance

The value and importance of peace of mind is difficult to quantify. A vacation is often a family-oriented investment in activities and new destinations that do lift the spirits and contribute to positive memories for a very long time. That whole experience should not be rudely disrupted and the money that was invested lost because of a missed flight, lost luggage, an urgent need to cancel due to death of a family member, or medical need in a foreign country where doctors and staff may not speak English. The alternative is to purchase travel insurance to cover the major issues that could disrupt your vacation in a very costly way. It is true that travel insurance is an elective expense, but it is a cost that is small relative to what  you might lose. For one thing, it is almost impossible to list all of the possible reasons your cruise or tour might be canceled, interrupted, or delayed. Not so ironically, travel insurance covers situations that are rarely, if ever, covered by your own health insurance or homeowner's insurance. The primary question is, "Could I lose the scheduled trip and the money paid out?" Regrettably, the answer can often be, "Yes." Worse, you could need medical air evacuation that could really set you back financially if you didn't have travel insurance.

Ubiquitous Security Screening for Airline Travel

The Transportation Security Administration (TSA) details recommendations related to security issues involving airlines on their website at www.tsa.gov. In addition to the most current comments and recommendations, you can go to the FAQ section to get more detailed information on what is not permissible to take in carry-on as well as checked luggage. One of the many items offered is a recognized locking mechanism to secure luggage yet allow inspection by authorized TSA personnel. Another alternative is to carry locking plastic bag ties that can be added to the luggage by TSA personnel after an inspection.

External bag straps on a carry-on bag can help to secure your luggage from a theft while waiting at the airport or dining in a restaurant. A related problem occurs periodically when a checked bag turns up missing and is never recovered. Airline insurance coverage for a lost bag tends to be grossly insufficient to cover the value of items such as expensive jewelry (which should never be in checked luggage). X-ray scans are perhaps a little too specific to get past the eyes of a determined baggage handler/thief. Moral: Consider taking imitation jewelry and wear it in secure settings. Also, be sure to allow extra time for inspections—especially for international travel, holiday travel, and flights that are fully booked. It may be the people just ahead of you in line that create a significant delay that impacts your schedule.

Prepare for Screening in Advance

If you are mentally prepared and know what to expect at airport security check points, you should be able to move through the process quickly. TSA personnel utilize a variety of screening techniques such as metal detectors, x-ray of all bags, and possible search of your person by hand wand. Shoes and all metallic objects such as keys, coins, watches, belt buckles, jewelry, cell phones, laptops, cameras, and purses are typically placed in a container to be x-rayed before proceeding to the departure gate. If desired, passengers do have the right to request a private screening, but there are no guarantees that everything will be done in a manner that is timely enough to remain on a tight schedule.

Increasing Surveillance

Security in certain public places like international airports usually includes surveillance cameras and trained staff who watch for atypical behavior, counterfeit passports, and other documents from the parking area to the final departure gates. For obvious reasons any weapons or objects with the potential to be used as a weapon (e.g., cigarette lighter and a can of lighter fluid) are strictly banned and subject to confiscation and/or personally detained. Law enforcement personnel must follow very exact procedures for transporting firearms. TSA has recently announced that scissors up to 4 inches in length will be allowed in carry-ons and shoes may be inspected less frequently. Security is expected to become more random than ever and may include bomb-sniffing dogs, more camera surveillance, and some form of biometrics.

Security for Children

Children will likely have their own possessions inspected such as toys, blankets, strollers, stuffed animals, shoes, bags, diapers, and so forth. In public places, especially with big crowds, it's wise to make arrangements with responsible people to help watch and to perhaps escort younger children of the opposite sex into restrooms, dressing rooms for the swimming pool, and any areas where the child would be out of sight. It's not enough to say, "He (or she) was only gone for a few seconds."

Preventing Illnesses

The potential for contagious diseases to be transported from any part of the world to another at the speed of a jet airliner has been a reality for some time. It can be anticipated that special screening precautions will be taken to limit the hazards of potentially lethal diseases such as avian flu. Occasionally, there has been a cruise ship alert issued for Norwalk virus (norovirus) which also

175

has flu-like symptoms. The U.S. Center for Disease Control and Prevention (CDC) has estimated that up to 23 million people in the U.S. are showing symptoms of the Norwalk virus each year. The same report indicates that less than one percent of all cruise passengers are contracting this flu-like illness. One reason for this difference is that most cruise ships now offer hand-sanitizing liquid dispensers outside of entrances for dining areas and embarkation stations. According to the CDC, the cruise lines maintain one of the highest standards for sanitation anywhere in the world. Staff on board cruise ships rigorously clean and disinfect all public areas around the clock. Cruise staff are especially attentive to door handles, railings, eating areas, and public restrooms. For further information visit the CDC website at www.cdc.gov.

The Importance of the Tour Guide

While in China, in 2005, this writer was met at the airport by one of three local tour guides recruited and trained by Viking River Cruises. The tour guide was our group's translator for the local language, customs, and laws. She provided a wealth of information and openly discussed local economics, entertainment, politics, religion, and topics of interest to a group of American tourists.

Our group was comfortably squired around in very modern tour buses, less modern bicycle rickshaws, and often on foot as our group mingled with other tourists and locals at the ancient Hutong village, the Great Wall of China, the Beijing Zoo, the hotel, the restaurants, Tiananmen Square, the bus stops and even the airport as the group transferred to other cities and the Yangtze River. There was quickly a bond that developed between the group and the 26-year-old tour guide that created the feeling that we would follow her anywhere. In one city, for instance, she said people do not walk on the grass of the city park. It was obvious enough from simple observation that no one was walking on the park grass and our group didn't either.

The same tour guide told us the story of the couple who took a taxi from the hotel to visit a famous site, or perhaps just to go out for dinner at a restaurant. On the return trip they handed a book of matches from their hotel to the taxi driver and used hand gestures and English that the driver did not understand to say they wanted to go back to that hotel. The taxi driver proceeded to take them to the factory where the matches were made. The passengers had failed to get the name of the hotel written down in Chinese characters that the taxi driver would understand. However, with some significant delays "the little problem" was worked out and they eventually got back to the correct hotel and, no, they are not still lost somewhere in China. The point is, our group was comfortable in following our tour guide virtually any place the guide wanted us to go. We didn't always have to have her in sight because we knew she was watching after the group and rounded us up as necessary from time to time. She also had good information on how to barter with street vendors and even where the best public restrooms were located.

Additional Sources of Information

www.airsafe.com
www.cigna.com
www.embassy.org
www.interpol.int
www.sierratradingpost.com
www.smartcardalliance.org
www.travelguard.com

www.travelguidenow.com
www.travelinsured.com
www.tsa.gov
www.usatoday.com/travel
www.virtuallythere.com
www.weather.com

23
Common Sense

Two roads diverged in a wood, and I– I took the one less traveled by, and that has made all the difference.

—Robert Frost

Get a Jump on the Holidays

Use the seasons, especially the transition from one season to another, to your advantage. One example is to plan a family gathering in early December to celebrate the holidays without the high cost and crowd crunch of Thanksgiving and Christmas/New Year's. The months of April and May are typically underused travel times because school is still in session. The weather is much improved and it is after spring break and before school's summer vacation. You can anticipate some great bargains. Hawaii, for instance, really needs your travel business at that time, but by June it is a totally different situation.

Travel Light–Period

Reducing the number of bags carried on each trip will reduce the amount of bag-handling tips each time you get in and out of a shuttle, a taxi, and a hotel. Less baggage may also reduce some delays and stress about possibly losing a bag or of appearing more affluent than you feel you are. When there is less luggage and weight limits are

not exceeded there is less chance of a bag becoming lost for one reason or another.

Casual, Not Risqué

Dress for comfort, not for special effect. Sometimes for men that may mean wearing a tuxedo (consider the courtroom scene in the film *My Cousin Vinny*). Mostly, it means respect for the people in the new destination. Be sensitive to how others may view both your style of dress and behavior on their turf. When off the beach and in public places, it may be inappropriate to wear a bikini, thong underwear that shows, a sleeveless blouse, short shorts, or flashy jewelry. Consider an inexpensive travel wristwatch. Non-logo clothing and shoes can sometimes be an advantage to reduce solicitations by street vendors and maybe to enhance your bartering position for making a purchase. The ideal is to not offend the sensibilities of local residents and local business people.

Horse-Trading Can Be Part of the Fun

Haggling over price with street vendors is often much more typical of distant locales than it is of the U.S. Consider offering up to one-third off the asking price unless you feel it is already very well priced. Be persistent and maybe start to walk away. In other

words, don't loiter over an item and ask lots of questions about it if you seriously expect a significant discount, and especially if you plan to walk away regardless of the final price. Art dealers and jewelry stores are generally found in some abundance at nearly every tourist destination and tend to be negotiable on the price. When you see something you really like, make a discounted offer and expect to do some give and take. In the few minutes that tend to be available, it may be possible to reach a mutual "meeting of the minds" for something that you may value for years to come. Rather than trivial souvenirs, it may be possible to buy a "personal treasure" at a very realistic discount. It helps, however, to avoid large objects that are heavy or awkward to carry, or fragile items such as cut glassware. One American traveler purchased cut glass items in Prague and had them shipped to the U.S. When the package was opened, many pieces of glass had been broken.

Deals on Wheels

When taking a taxi, ask the price and agree to that price before getting into the car, or just walk away. This works best when the driver is not strictly using a meter. If the quoted price is acceptable, have the correct payment in advance, and pay after exiting from the taxi. Some taxi drivers claim they are no longer able (or willing) to make change. Often, you can assume the tip has already been factored into the price unless you feel the service was extraordinary. As you ride along, you may want to discreetly record the driver's name and identification information. After the vacation is over, it will be possible to send a compliment or a complaint to the taxi company depending on the quality of service received. Another option is to negotiate a group fare in advance with a taxi driver who has a van-like type of taxi. Agree to a price per person for your group of four or five persons to be chauffeured exclusively for an estimated period of time with payment to be made on completion of the agreement, not in advance.

Thieves Love Carry-ons

Carry-on bags with small wheels and detachable shoulder straps can be very functional yet should be readily identifiable since so many appear the same. The long strap works well to actually stand on or lop around your leg (or a chair leg) when you are distracted at the ticket desk, a vendor stop, eating place, waiting place, or restroom. Reminder: Theft is rarely a problem for travelers who remain part of a group, tour, or cruise, if they exercise good common sense about possessions and personal conduct. Missing out on the experience and personal memories of a vacation journey because of concern about a possible minor loss is itself a form of theft. Procrastinate, and time becomes a thief. Plan your trips and let time work for you.

Long Flights

If you are going to use the airline's pillow, consider bringing your own pillowcase. You can also pack your own washable lap-blanket instead of maybe paying a fee to use the airline's. When on long flight segments, it can be helpful to take off your shoes and put on an extra pair of socks. This writer's feet always seem to swell during air travel. For very long international flights you can wear compression socks that come up to your knees and do help with swelling and discomfort. For such flights, it also helps to minimize the objects that go in front of your seat and to place belongings in the nearest overhead compartment. One slight risk factor is that if you must be relocated to some other part of the plane, there is the chance that your property may be accidentally removed by someone else. Aisle seats also become much more attractive on long flights because of the potential to get up and stretch your legs or get to the restroom without first disturbing the passenger(s) next to you. Air travel is really about the destination, not the chair.

Additional Sources of Information

www.fodors.com
www.frommers.com
www.kaboose.com
www.studyabroad.rutgers.edu
www.thereareplaces.com
www.travellady.com
www.travel-wisdom.com
www.usatoday.com/travel
www.virtualtourist.com
www.womenstravelclub.com

24
Clothing and Packing

*Why buy good luggage? You only use it
when you travel.* —Yogi Berra

Lighter Is Better

Much has been written about the virtues of traveling light. For many years the trend has been moving from formal to informal and, with respect to international travel in particular, is often described as resort, cruise, or country club casual. Shorts that have zippered or Velcro pockets and can also double as swim suits have many uses and take up little space. The ideal type of clothing to have dries quickly and can be hand washed, if desired, and used again and again without carrying duplicates. One such option is the zip-off pants that can be converted to shorts. Solution: Pack light. Smaller and fewer bags can mean less hassle, fewer tips, and less travel discomfort. You can accomplish that goal in part with multi-functional clothing, careful folding (takes less space), and tight packing in zip-lock plastic bags that allow the air to be forced out. "Less is more," but your basic motto could be M.O.R.E. (miniaturize, organize, reduce and economize).

Travel-Smart Clothes

Darker and mixed colors tend to be more forgiving of travel spills from eating and drinking on the move. Denim is one of those fabrics and colors that typically travels well without looking wrinkled or soiled except when pushed to extremes. Denim has become a universal fabric seen around the world and may be fine for many situations, but usually looks overly casual for evening wear and is even banned by many quality restaurants at dinner time. One option to packing formal wear is to rent a tuxedo for the wedding party or formal dinner and photo opportunity aboard a cruise ship. Men can save quite a bit of space by simply renting the black dress shoes.

Travel Hats, Jackets and Accessories

A crushable hat, such as a Canadian Tilley hat, likewise packs readily and as a result may have much more utility than a hard-formed hat. Baseball hats are classics for travel for basically the same reasons. A light-weight windbreaker has great utilitarian value, takes up little luggage space, and can actually keep you quite warm when zipped up except in very cold conditions. Leather jackets can be an option but tend to be much heavier than nylon or synthetic fibers and can be quite bulky to pack. Gore-Tex clothing may be another option for light weight and high versatility.

Layer, Layer, Layer

Consider layering garments if needed for some additional warmth rather than including a bulky coat. Likewise, avoid bulky sweaters that take up lots of space and may not even be worn unless a snow-sport vacation is involved. A few minutes of shivering while waiting for a taxi, shuttle, or some other brief situation will likely be an advantage to carrying an extra bulky jacket.

When reasonable, avoid multiple styles such as formal wear, informal wear, sailing clothes, climbing clothes, rain gear, cold weather clothing, and tropical clothing. Dressing for high heat does not necessarily ensure that there will be hot or even extra warm days at the time you actually travel. The typically brief inconveniences of being too hot, too cold, or too wet, however, are minor compared to the severe inconveniences of transporting "too much stuff" everywhere you go.

Lots of Pockets, Easy Wash, Quick Dry

Garments with lots of pockets, maybe even concealed interior pockets, tend to be a real asset for travel and reduce the reliance on extra bags. Polyesters have a tendency to hold odors and may dry more slowly than natural fibers. Microfiber garments can be a good choice because they can be washed easily and dry quickly. Laundromats can also be very helpful but will likely cost more than a few quarters. A good general precaution is to not leave the laundromat until your clothes are finished. Unattended clothing has a real potential to disappear. The major advantage is that you can pack far less clothing and still have clean, fresh clothing, and feel comfortable about how you look. Socks and other things can possibly be hand washed and dried overnight. Local cleaners, and especially cruise ship laundries, can also clean and press select items for a reasonable price.

The Ubiquitous T-shirt

T-shirts, often sold in the range of three for $10, are a ubiquitous trade item that can be found in virtually every part of the tourist world. The lowest-cost shirts are generally screen-printed and the upper-end shirts are embroidered and often sell for more than the screen-printed variety. The low-end shirts typically shrink by at least a size or two and are sometimes described as grandfather/ grandson shirts. That is, after granddad washes and dries the shirt it will only fit his grandson. The idea is to have fun. Buy a number of souvenir shirts and wear them for the fun of it before they need to be washed and shrink in the dryer. This choice can be a supplement to your travel wardrobe.

Tropical Footwear

Sandals pack well and provide excellent air circulation for your feet in warm and hot climates and even in very confined environments such as aircraft cabins. Slip-on water shoes are another great alternative to basic flip-flops (thongs) and are good foot protection for beaches, lakes, swimming pools, locker rooms, and even walking down the hallway to and from the hot tub or spa. Shoes account for a major amount of bulk. Minimize where possible and tend to wear good traction athletic shoes while in transit and on and off tours. Socks and other items can often be stuffed inside shoes to utilize that space. A thin pair of thongs or water shoes can be excellent for hot beaches, pools, hot tubs, showers, and some protection from getting a foot injury or disease. Some athletic shoes are far less bulky than others. In the short term, less is more.

Cross Pack

Divide up clothing, medications, and cosmetics among different pieces of luggage. Then, if one bag is lost each person still has some change of clothes and can cover basic needs without an urgent rush to the pharmacy or clothing store. Goal: Take less than you need, not more. Look for the miniaturized version of nearly everything you pack. A very good way to ensure that your luggage arrives when you do is to confirm the three-letter designation (airport code) that is placed on each piece of checked luggage. You will want to be absolutely sure that the final destination of your baggage matches your own. Simply verify the airline destination codes with the airline before departure so you can visually confirm where your luggage is going. In a rush, mistakes are made at check-in and it can be intensely frustrating to get somewhere and not have one or more pieces of luggage.

Airline Overhead Compartments May Be Shrinking

Another way to generate more airline revenue is to limit the size, number, and weight of carry-on bags as well as checked bags. To avoid major frustrations and possibly substantial penalties, be sure to verify sizes and weights allowed for each airline you will be using. Over-packing can still make it difficult or impossible to use the carry-on space provided. Be especially careful with the weight of luggage to be checked. Alaska Airlines has imposed a weight penalty since October 1, 2003. That is, checked bags from 50 to 71 pounds are assessed a $25 surcharge. Bags from 71 to 100 pounds are assessed $50. Penalties up to $150+ are possible.

Underpack

Consider disposable clothing. Flexible, thin clothing can be layered, if necessary, for brief cold spells (most travel tends to be within heated or cooled areas). Easy wash-and-wear materials can be hand washed and dried quickly, or laundered in transit. If you run critically short on something, consider buying a souvenir shirt, shorts, or even simple footwear. There must be some reason that clothing stores are so prevalent everywhere you go. Allow space for the inevitable gifts that are purchased for family, friends, and yourself that simply cannot be found at an import store near your home. Even luggage can be simplified. Remove long straps from checked luggage that could possibly snag on unfriendly conveyor belts. Avoid or carefully pack items that can break easily with rough handling and be sure to mark each bag in ways that are easily recognizable as yours alone. Plastic tie straps can be a great way to lock bags and still allow easy access if the bag needs to be inspected. Mostly, keep everything possible light, compact, versatile, and replaceable in the case of a loss.

Luggage Grows and Grows

Consider a class on efficient packing ideas and highly compact, multi-purpose travel products. One common rule of travel is that baggage usually expands proportionately to the time you are away and the number of purchase stops you make. Buying gifts for others is one of the most common pastimes for people when they travel. The number and types of vendors at virtually every stop are a testament to that assumption. Also consider the possibility of shipping excess baggage (especially dirty clothes and surplus shoes) by UPS, DHL, or others such as Cruise Shippers, a WFLLC Company. See their website and then consider this alternative for traveling light. Contact Ray Walters, Chairman, at www.raywalters@cruiseshippers.net. Florida: 4153 SW 47th Ave. #125, Fort Lauderdale, FL 33314, or Alaska: 617 Willoughby, Juneau, AK 99801.

Light Clothing Is Usually Right

Consider a water-resistant windbreaker and rain hat for each traveler as compact ways to cope with periodic intervals of cool or wet weather. Such items take up little space, don't need to be "wrinkle-free," and are for traveler comfort. A black outfit will tend to be appropriate for the more formal occasions and doesn't have to be bulky. In general, try to avoid clothing with metal objects that tend to trigger airport security alarms, or that readily show spots or stains such as some silk or suede fabrics. Avoid extra tight or extra loose clothing that can either be uncomfortable for long sitting, or potentially snag on something that could result in injury.

Dressing to get attention makes more sense in private than in public places. Dressing for casual comfort as a tourist makes lots of sense and adds to travel enjoyment.

Minimize and Avoid Trauma

Consider one versatile sports coat or dressy dress that will serve many purposes. Likewise, consider disposable underclothing, disposable anything, and items that can possibly be shipped back if the overall amount of luggage becomes too cumbersome. Plastic raingear that folds down to the size of a wallet is ideal. A crushable hat is sometimes ideal for travel. It can be worn as a sun hat, a rain hat, and even be a place to stash an extra bit of cash, or back-up identification. Umbrellas are typically too bulky to pack and carry. For the occasional rainy day it may make more sense to alter activities than to be totally prepared. Finally, consider using a traveler's checklist to ensure that you have what you really need in the most compact format or style, and not more.

Additional Sources of Information

www.cil.com

www.cotswoldoutdoor.com

www.christinecolumbus.com

www.exofficio.com

www.freetraveltips.com

www.independenttraveler.com

www.magellans.com

www.new-list.com

www.normthompson.com

www.organize-everything.com

www.packinglight.com

www.packitup.com

www.tilley.com

www.travelessentials.com

www.travelpod.com

www.travelsmith.com

www.usoutdoorstore.com

25
Time Savers

Take only memories, leave only footprints. —Chief Seattle
(Namesake for City of Seattle)

• Be frugal with time as if it were money—often, it is difficult to separate the two. One of the most valued attributes of travel, however, is to experience time in a different way. Break away from routines that may be externally imposed. Set new time frames that are exciting, distinctive, and definitely out of the ordinary. "Seize the day." Let time ooze, flow, and ebb in ways that it has not been doing. Measure time by the beautiful sunrises and sunsets rather than the hands of a watch. Have leisurely, not rushed meals, and walk or use conveyances that are completely away from any possible freeway. Stop and smell the roses, the bougainvillea, or the salt air.

• Getting started, however, likely means getting to the airport on time. Allow ample time to get to the airport early or extra early. Anticipate possible delays on the way to the airport, delays in parking or returning a rental car, and delays in getting the needed shuttle. One of the last things you will want is to be held back by freeway accidents that can tie up a route to the airport for hours. When keeping any schedule or appointment, allow generous amounts of time and consider routes that may not be as fast as the freeway but that do offer flexibility in case of a traffic jam.

• Self-service kiosks at airports are becoming much more commonplace and may help you to avoid long lines inside the terminal. Curbside baggage check-ins can also be a time saver when it is simply not possible to get everything into carry-on bags. Something new to watch is that many airlines are beginning to assess a "per bag" handling charge for curbside check-in.

• Being at the airport early may be the best way to avoid long lines (queue). It is possible that you may be standing in the wrong line and likely to be even more frustrated when you finally get the "correct" line. When you are outside of the U.S., it is sometimes difficult to determine which is the "correct line."

• It can be very helpful to use airline websites and/or airline 800 numbers to confirm arrival and departure schedules, gate information, and perhaps details about weather, rental car, and hotel details. Delayed flights can waste your valuable time and result in missed connections. It also pays to be cautious about very tight connecting times especially when you may have to go significant distances from one terminal to another, or when you have critical ship or tour departure times. If connections are tight it may be wise to book air transportation that has been blocked (reserved) by the cruise line rather than book air on your own. In case of emergencies, the cruise line or tour company can be of assistance in making alternate arrangements.

• Avoid wrapping packages that will be carried in your luggage. It is easier to wrap gifts after you get home than to wait while each package is opened for possible inspection.

• Be sure to charge your laptop battery or digital camera batteries before departure. A good way to save e-mail time is to compose letters and documents in a word processing format and send as an attachment, or copy into an e-mail message in a matter of seconds when you must pay to go online.

• Be aware of possible U.S. government travel advisory warnings from the State Department when considering overseas travel. If a notice is issued to avoid a particular area, you may not be able to obtain travel insurance for that specific area.

• Holiday time savers: Consider doing most holiday shopping before you travel and minimize the holiday/vacation time spent standing around in long lines. Allow extra time to off-set the inevitable holiday crowds. Arrive early and perhaps carry something to read. Magazines and paperbacks are ideal because they don't necessarily have to be returned. They can be recycled.

• Consider temporary expansion of cell phone service to cover areas where you will be traveling. However, remote areas may not have cell towers to allow the phone to work. Another option may be www.skype.com where you can convert your laptop into a national and international telephone at great, low rates. Be sure to work out the details before you depart. The cost savings can be phenomenal compared to a marine band phone call.

• Use a credit or debit card with your photograph on the card for making purchases. If you are traveling outside of the U.S., credit card and debit card purchases avoid getting change in a foreign currency that may be tedious or costly to convert. Pre-purchase stamps to avoid long lines at the post office during the holiday season, or pay the desk clerk to stamp and mail your cards and letters. Be sure to purchase appropriate stamps if being mailed from a destination outside of the U.S.

• Continental breakfast, or the equivalent that can be purchased at a grocery store, saves time, cost, tipping, and morning delays that can upset the remainder of a day. Many properties will offer a continental breakfast to help start your day. Consider one light meal periodically, especially at breakfast or the occasional dinner to save time, money, put more flexibility into your travel day, and save a few calories.

• Minimize the potentially long security inspections. International air carriers recommend getting to the airport from 2-3 hours prior to departure. Domestic carriers often recommend 1-2 hours before departure because of typically crowded flights and variable security inspections of each passenger. Security checks may not delay you but the people in front of you may cause real havoc with an otherwise tight schedule. Carry-on bags can facilitate transfer to an earlier flight, and actually avoid waiting for baggage claim after arrival.

• Verify that you have a full, legal connection for each plane change. Transferring to a different air carrier can be especially troublesome when there are long distances from one terminal to another. Many airports have motorized transportation within the airport terminal.

• Red-eye flights can eliminate the cost of an overnight hotel stay and an additional shuttle or taxi fare. However, sleep quality on such flights may be very poor and flight delays could add real stress to your day in being on time to board your cruise or another flight at the other end.

• Consider a one-night stay at a hotel near the airport before your vacation flight. Many hotels now offer free or low-cost Park n' Fly programs if you pay for one night (even if you do not actually stay there for the night). Creatively work out your own parking solutions and save. Paying someone a nominal fee to drive you to the airport is possibly the most creative idea. Also, keep in mind that taxis may be more prompt and precise about where you are dropped off, but will generally cost a lot more than a shuttle service.

• Like Murphy's Law, which basically says something can always go wrong, when you are getting ready under pressure, there seems to always "be one more detail." Follow a travel checklist. Consider Yahoo Maps or Mapquest and related Internet sources that can provide step-by-step travel instructions. Allow more than ample time in getting to the airport, carry bottled water and snacks such as nutrition bars, so you can possibly bypass a restaurant if in a hurry, and in *no time* your vacation begins.

26
Your Travel Rights

It is awfully important to know what is and what is not your business. —Gertrude Stein

Rule 240 (Formerly Airline Rule 240)

Consider the basics of airline Rule 240 for handling individual cases of extended flight delay or cancellation. The DOT requires airlines to keep a Rule 240 copy available for passengers at every ticket counter. But don't' count on it. The original airline has an obligation to make every effort to get a qualifying, delayed passenger on the next available flight even if a move up in "class of seating" is required.

This airline rule can require an original airline to transfer a qualifying passenger to another airline to facilitate a timely continuation of a delayed or cancelled flight that is not due to "force majeure" events: weather, strikes, "acts of God," or other occurrences that the airlines say they cannot control. Airline options can also include meal and hotel vouchers.

Ticket transfers may be available only among the major carriers and typically do not include smaller, discount carriers, or charter flights. Passengers should therefore avoid overly tight schedules if delays would produce negative consequences. Confirm flight schedules well in advance if serious delays would be problematic. Verify, if necessary, that an e-ticket can be transferred without first being converted to a paper ticket. Ideally, avoid flight scheduling that is so tight that virtually any delay would produce negative results such as a missed cruise.

When traveling by air, you should carry with you a copy of the airline's Rule 240. If you feel you are entitled to compensation under this rule, simply use the phrase," Rule 240" and show your copy of the rule. If the ticket counter person is unwilling to help, ask for a supervisor. You will eventually get someone's attention and hopefully a solution for your dilemma. A major airline may be required to issue a full refund of the unused portion of a ticket if an acceptable alternative flight cannot be obtained.

Airlines are not required to guarantee their schedules. If connections, such as catching a cruise ship, are critical, it may be far safer to arrive one or more days in advance than to be completely stressed with an airline that could not control the weather, or other potentials for delay. Often, you can increase your odds with early morning travel. Fewer of those flights tend to get backed up as the possible complications of the day build more and more pressure on the airline and other passenger carriers.

Know Your Rights

For additional information, consider the following sources: *Travel Rights: Know the Rules of the Road and Air Before You Go* by Charlie Leocha, *The Travel Detective* by Peter Greenberg, or go to information websites such as www.smarterliving.com and www.mytravelrights.com. Typically, most vacation plans, especially

packaged programs, are developed for entertainment purposes only, and it will rarely be necessary to litigate your traveler's legal rights. Each traveler right that exists in the U.S. or Canada will not be identical in foreign destinations and the potential for remedies will certainly be different unless you are willing to remain at that location for an extended period of time to resolve a possible financial loss.

Be Sensitive to Workers You Meet Along the Way

Crossing a labor dispute picket line is an individual decision. Airlines and other employers both domestically and internationally can be in the midst of a strike as you travel. Alternate sources can be used in some instances or a ticket might be cancelled until a later date. Being flexible and considerate of workers in a dispute may be all that you can do. Showing respect for people who are working to make your vacation experience more pleasurable is usually well received.

Freedom to Travel Without "Showing Your Papers"

For a rousing discussion of the U.S. government's right to demand identification documents prior to travel in response to the 9/11 tragedy, see the July 18, 2002, court case, Gilmore v. Ashcroft at www.cryptome.org/freetotravel.htm. John Gilmore argues that honest citizens have the right to travel throughout the U.S. without undue interference by the government unless that citizen is reasonably suspected of committing a crime. The "issue" is understood to be unresolved. Basically, be prepared to show government-issued photo-ID when you travel by air or train. Be prepared to show your passport to cross international borders. Be especially cautious about the rules if you suddenly have a new married name, or change of name, and official ID that does not document that change. This can be especially important for boarding commercial airliners and for use of a passport to exit or re-enter the U.S.

Laws and Rights Are Not the Same Everywhere

International law can be an enormous and excessively complicated subject. The reality is that well-funded travel vendors will rarely, if ever, put their clientele at risk of violating any of the local laws as a result of chance or ignorance. The assumption, of course, is that travelers are not using falsified documents and not involved in activities that might be taken as illegal activity within almost any jurisdiction. U.S. and Canadian embassy offices are typically available as a resource in the case of a lost passport or assertion of one's legal rights. It is only in the rarest of known instances that legal representation may need to be retained by vacation travelers in a foreign country. One understanding is that major cruise lines typically have foreign registries and conduct most of their services in international waters that are subject to international law. Fortunately, vacation travel for an estimated 10 million international cruisers from the United States each year has resulted in almost no legal issues that have gathered major media attention. Each vacation traveler who meets face to face with citizens of another country helps to build positive links toward economic development between diverse nationalities. Good fences may make good neighbors, but it is travel that keeps the gates open.

27
Travel Vignettes

We wander for distraction, but we travel for fulfillment.
—Hilaire Belloc

Travel throughout the world has been one of the most fulfilling experiences of this writer's life. I have relished the learning experience of nearly two dozen cruises, plus domestic car and motorhome trips throughout the U.S. and Canada, and land-based trips in Europe and Asia that have taken me nearly around the world several times. I have ventured as far north as Coldfoot, Alaska, in a motorhome; snorkeled in the coral beds of Roatan, Honduras; gone swimming in the South China Sea off Borneo; walked on a portion of the Great Wall of China; climbed the Mayan Temple of Kukulcan, the largest pyramid at Chichen-Itza, in Mexico's Yucatan Peninsula; and toured the spectacular Hermitage Art Museum of St. Petersburg, Russia. Since retiring from a career as a school teacher, I have been actively involved as a travel consultant. The focus now is on assisting my clients in planning and implementing vacation experiences that are intended to exceed their expectations. The following is a brief summary of my favorite travel experiences and some special features that may be of interest to the active traveler:

Hawaiian Islands

You don't have to read James Michener's book, *Hawaii,* to feel the irresistible charm and diversity of the Hawaiian Islands. The near-perfect climate year around (the Trade Winds do bring some showers) combines with surf, sand, and distinctive cultural

influences to offer a paradise-like experience to those who seek it. The islands were first inhabited by ocean-going voyagers from the Marqueses Islands who continue to leave their indelible imprint. Current attractions include viewing the Kilauea volcano and black sand beaches of the Big Island (Hawaii). You can view local arts and crafts under a giant banyan tree in the former whaling village of Lahaina on Maui, visit art galleries, or maybe observe the sunrise at Haleakala Crater. Drive the winding road to Hana, watch the migration of whales, attend a Polynesian luau, ride in a glass-bottomed boat, surf, dive, or snorkel in tropical waters, or just enjoy the moment along miles and miles of sandy beaches.

Oahu offers the contrast of a metropolitan area, Waikiki Beach, the Royal Hawaiian Hotel, Pearl Harbor Memorial, USS Missouri, hiking in a tropical rainforest of the interior, Polynesian Cultural Center, and great surfing. Kauai, "The Garden Isle," offers beach resorts, golf, and great scenic views such as the Waimea Canyon, the Grand Canyon of the Pacific, which is best viewed by helicopter ride. Molokai, famed for the Old Hawaiian style of life, has mule and horseback trips, great resorts, and wonderful trails for biking and hiking. Lanai has its own feel with distinctive resorts, scenic views along the Munro Trail, and pristine sandy beaches. You can simply enjoy the experience of being in paradise and being a part of the "Aloha spirit." Hawaii has some of the best beaches, golf, shopping, and restaurants to be found anywhere.

Mexican Riviera, Yucatan, and Riviera Maya

The sunny coastal regions of Mexico and Central America are major attractions throughout the entire year. These destinations are readily accessible by cruise ship or a combination of air and

resort hotel packages. Sunny weather, beautiful beaches, and the distinctive cultures of Mexico and Latin America come together with the hospitality and adventure of vacationing "south of the border." On the western coast there is the Baja Peninsula with the blue-green Sea of Cortes on one side and the mighty Pacific Ocean on the other. Top-quality resorts and golf courses are common in the Los Cabos region. Along the west coast are the exciting destinations of Mazatlan, Puerto Vallarta, Ixtapa-Zihuatanejo, and Acapulco. Consider an inland bus tour of rural communities in the Sierra Madre Mountains. Visit the colonial city of Guadalajara.

On the Caribbean or southeastern side of Mexico is the resort island of Cozumel. Along the Yucatan Peninsula are Cancun, Tulum, Xcaret, and traces of the ancient Mayan culture that extend southward into the Riviera Maya and Belize region. Tour Mayan ruins and learn more of their history past and present as you

enjoy the distinctiveness of pre-Columbian and Latin culture. Each destination of Mexico has its own unique tropical feel, colonial or contemporary history, and warm hospitality. English is commonly spoken and understood in most of the well-traveled areas and it is an opportunity to experience their delight as you speak a few words of their language. Sample the great food in the many fine restaurants. I have occasionally had a flavored Tequila Margarita made from the agave plant, been serenaded by a strolling mariachi band, and observed iguanas and tropical birds up close in their natural habitat. You can too.

Cruise through Germany on the Rhine and Main Rivers

From the river, I observed castles, vineyards, scenic small towns, historic sites, the diversity of riverboat traffic, unique bridges, and postcard images of Central Europe. Most of the goods used by

the local residents are delivered by barge. Many of these barges are individually owned and the barge itself may be the home for a family. Some of the barges carried a personal car, children's play equipment, and perhaps even a clothes line to dry their clothes.

Soon, the cruise ship arrived at the historic city of Cologne. This city on the Rhine is perhaps most famous for the twin-towered Gothic cathedral that dates to the 14th century and was spared from Allied bombing during WWII in part because the twin spires were a directional indicator for pilots on both sides. The historic attractions of that restored city date back to remnants of Roman occupation when the town was known as Colonia Agrippina. Places visited included the original bottling facility for "eau de cologne" (originally a medication), a Kolsch

beer bar, and the Cologne Chocolate Factory. I visited fascinating small towns on a daily basis and found friendly shopkeepers everywhere.

Vienna

As the capital of Austria, Vienna has long been a crossroad for culture, trade, music, and even political power in Central Europe for thousands of years. Located along the Danube River, which was the northernmost boundary for the Roman Empire in that region, Vienna is both a modern metropolis and an historic treasure trove. The influences of many different cultures and the evolution of Christianity are evident in the architecture, palaces, cathedrals, and museums. Historic traces back to the Middle Ages can be readily found. View 500 years of the Hapsburg dynasty and the opulence of Schonbrunn Palace, hear the Vienna Boys Choir, visit the Opera House, and see the Lipizzaner Stallions of the Spanish Riding School of Vienna. Additional major

points of interest include the St. Stephen's Cathedral, Hotel Sacher, and Vienna's 100-year-old subway system which is safe and very convenient to use.

Sample the great Viennese cuisine which is different from German cuisine. Consider the local wines and fine dining in the Grinsing District, or more raucous meals and entertainment in the "Bermuda Triangle" bar area (so named because when you go in, you won't want to come out). Music is the lifeblood of Vienna with frequent Strauss and Mozart festivals, concerts, and operas. Taste the wiener schnitzel and fine wines. Beer and sausage as an evening meal is what the Viennese call fast food and it is usually sold by street vendors during the summer months. For additional sightseeing consider the historic town of Salzburg, the birthplace of Mozart, and gateway to the Alps. It is located 300 km to the west of Vienna and is surrounded by beautiful countryside.

St. Petersburg, Russia

Perhaps the most familiar attraction of this showplace city founded by Peter the Great 300 years ago is the Hermitage Museum. Located in the Winter Palace of former czarist Russia, the ornate and rambling facility contains the world's largest art collection, and rivals the Louvre of Paris and El Prado of Madrid. Additional attractions for this beautiful, neo-classical metropolis on the Neva River include Russian Orthodox churches, Matrishka dolls, ballets, concerts, and the great Russian spirit of dancing, folk music, vodka, and costumes. Near the Hermitage is the battleship Aurora, which fired the first shot of the October 1917 Revolution.

The local humor is that the same gun now points directly at the former KGB offices. St. Petersburg is a must-see destination that was once inaccessible. While in the vicinity, additional priorities to visit are the Scandinavian capitals of Helsinki, Stockholm, and Oslo. Not to be missed are the medieval as well as contemporary cities of Tallinn (Estonia), Gdansk (Poland), and Copenhagen (Denmark). A recommended way to make that possible is to consider a Baltic cruise during the favorable weather of the summer months.

Yangtze River Cruise (2004)

As part of a brief stay in Beijing, I toured the city, the Great Wall, the Beijing Zoo, rode in two-person rickshaws through an ancient Hutong village within the city, and strolled around Tiananmen Square. From Beijing I traveled by air upstream on the Yangtze River and boarded a new Viking River Cruise Ship at Chongqing. From there, I traveled downstream through majestic river valleys toward the Three Gorges Dam (world's largest at 1.3 miles wide, 610 feet high, and 32 generators). The dam is scheduled for completion in 2009 and involves the re-settlement of ap-

proximately two million people. Along the way it was apparent how much the river has risen and, by the dam's completion, will rise to about 175 meters in some places. I observed the new cities that are mostly completed and well  above the projected new water line and away from the floods that have ravaged thousands of villages over the past 5,000 years. I heard that a major portion of the dam expense has been going to relocation of all affected villages and antiquities along more than 1,000 miles of the Yangtze River. I was amazed to learn that the

 city of Chongqing is one of the largest cities in the world with over 31 million residents and I had never heard of it until this trip. In addition to visiting several rebuilt cities along the Yangtze River, I sampled excellent food and briefly visited the

stunning city of Shanghai at the mouth of the Yangtze before flying home.

Malaysia

As the capital of the very prosperous and independent nation of Malaysia, Kuala Lumpur is noted for the Petronas Towers, the tallest twin towers in the world at 452 meters (the tallest buildings, incidentally, are the Sears Tower at 527 meters and the Taipei 101 at 508 meters). The capital's name literally means "River of Money" and prosperity is evident among the modern buildings, busy freeways, international shopping, a good standard of living for its residents. Manufacturing, international trade, and financial services are replacing the old economies of rubber trees and mining. The area is the world's largest manufacturer of pewter objects. Just to the south is the newly completed, planned city of Putrajaya, a model for this technologically advanced Islamic state. It is 19 square miles in size and contains elaborate tile mosques, a man-made lake with fountains, a suspension bridge, and is surrounded by experimental agriculture projects. The plan is for all government buildings to move from Kuala Lumpur to Putrajaya. Still further to the south is the ancient city of Malacca, which has been famous as the "Spice Island" of the Portuguese and Dutch traders since the early 1500's. Currently the city's oldest areas are a major center for antique shops. The harbor contains a replica of an old Dutch trading ship.

The peninsula region of Malaysia exhibited signs of prosperity everywhere. All of the areas visited appeared to be clean, healthy, vibrant, and a tropical garden area free of graffiti or other signs of decay. The northern region of the country is predominantly of Muslim faith. Further south and across from Singapore is the non-peninsula portion of Malaysia on the island of Borneo. That region is far more rural and extensively covered with mountainous jungle. It is also the home of an orangutan preserve that was very exciting to visit. The region is predominantly of the Catholic faith, agriculturally based, and has beautiful resorts along the South China Sea.

Fiji

Fiji is made up of over 300 islands in this South Pacific archipelago. Many are unoccupied or have only one small resort. The tropical feel is exquisite. One of the first images you are likely to have is that of the crystal clear water and a sense of quiet and a relaxed atmosphere. The U.S. dollar has a favorable exchange rate for Fijian dollars and the local residents are fluent in English. The welcome received from the Fijian people was fantastic. The most common expression you will hear is "bula" (boo-lah). The greeting means hello and a lot more. From the airport in Nadi (pronounced "nawn-dee") you may proceed to one of the large resorts on the main island that have all of the customary amenities, check in, and start a day of relaxation. Next, you

will likely want to proceed to one of the outer islands by air or boat to soak up the tropical atmosphere, check into a small resort, and explore all of the possibilities for water sports, visit a village, or find peaceful relaxation the way you want it to be.

Fiji may be three movies and three meals away from Los Angeles but it is definitely one of the world's best vacation values and filled with experiences that you will never forget. One of the not-so-secret facts about Fiji is that the islands are a favorite destination for Australian vacationers.

Tahiti

Thanks to the French artist, Paul Gauguin, and others who wrote about the South Pacific, Tahiti has a particular beauty and appeal that is best summed up with the word "paradise." Both French and Tahitian are the local languages and English is readily understood in many places, especially at the resorts and markets. The native culture has strong French influences and the local tourist economy is notable for high to very high prices. Anticipate spending more money than at other tropical destinations and savor the Tahitian experience. One of the first discoveries you make could be over-the-water bungalows combined with "Tahitian television." You remove the top of the coffee table and watch the colorful tropical fish below. You can expect fresh flowers everywhere, on your pillow, in the bathroom, replaced with new fresh flowers each day. The major islands of French Polynesia include Tahiti, Moorea, Raiatea, Bora Bora, Huahine, Manihi, Rangiroa, and Tahaa. Each has multiple resorts and each resort is a destination in itself. My favorite contrast of cultures occurred when our travel group arrived by boat at our resort in Huahine. The bellman came out to greet us wearing only a very short sulu (sarong), a woven reed hat, and blowing the conch shell. I was just beginning to get into the Tahiti spirit. I was wearing a tropical dress and the fresh vegetable and reed lei I had been given at the airport. Then, the bellman turned around and there was a cell phone clipped to the waist of his sulu.

Spain and Morocco

My experience in Spain was largely confined to the Costa del Sol (the Mediterranean coast of Spain). I can still recall sitting on the beach, soaking up the sun during a Spring vacation break, and thinking that the ocean was to the north, not the south as it actually was. The harbor was active with boats of all types and some of the most expensive-looking yachts that I have ever seen anywhere. I took several day trips during that week that included a flea market near Marbella, the Alhambra, the island of Gibraltar, and escorted tours to Tangier, Morocco. That part of North Africa is especially noted for good buys on leather goods and hand-woven carpets.

One of the memorable sights was a North African businessman with full Islamic-style clothing who was obviously also wearing a dark, pin-striped suit and wing-tip shoes.

Alaska, Victoria, and Vancouver B.C.

As a travel destination, Alaska can be thought of as two distinct areas. There is Southeastern Alaska where the major cruise ships sail from late spring to early fall, and there is the interior with the best-known attractions being Denali State Park, Fairbanks, and pristine hunting, fishing, and camping areas. Alaska is known for its magnificent snow-covered mountains and wilderness areas with abundant wildlife, lakes, and rivers. Southeastern Alaska actually borders western Canada, but you can only get to Ketchikan, Juneau, Wrangell, Sitka, or Petersburg by water or air. Each of these distinctive regions has its own Alaskan flavor. In Ketchikan, see

the lumberjack show and salmon runs so thick you can almost walk on their backs. In Juneau, ride the Mt. Roberts tram 1,800 feet above the harbor for scenic views, restaurant, and shopping. Try a beer at the Red Dog Saloon or maybe see humpback whales like we did. By chance, our "flight-seeing" trip in a float plane was cancelled due to rain, so we opted for a whale-watch boat. The rains were heavy that day and we mostly had to stay inside the boat, but we saw whale activity that was so spectacular that the naturalist onboard became totally excited and we all disregarded the rain. Mother whales and their calves were playing and putting on a great show for us. Everyone, especially the naturalist onboard, was taking all of the pictures that she could.

Victoria, the most British city west of England, is located at the southern tip of Vancouver Island in British Columbia. This elegant harbor city feels like a slice of the British Isles. There is the grandeur of the Empress Hotel which is a focal point as you approach the city from the water. The hotel is also notable for serving high tea in the afternoon and for having exterior lights that compliment the exterior lights on the parliament buildings and give the city an exquisite image at night. Local museums have outstanding archeological, ethnological, and historic exhibits. We

recently viewed the hand-written journals of Leonardo da Vinci in which he wrote and illustrated his inventions as if seen in a vision. First-time visitors should also consider a city tour on an English-style double-decker bus and the excellent seafood options at local restaurants, or bar and grill. Shopping has a distinct English feel along Government Street and the various side streets. Weather permitting, Bastion Square in the same area has many local artisans at an outdoor market. Be sure to try the local pubs to share in the really friendly spirit, great food, and sample the music of this very international community. If time allows, consider a short trip north to Butchart Gardens.

Vancouver, B.C. is a sophisticated, international-feeling city with great shopping, excellent hotels, Stanley Park, Granville Island, and a tram that takes you up Grouse Mountain and overlooks this beautiful harbor city. Many cruise ships sail to Alaska from Vancouver, B.C., to Far Eastern destinations, or south along the west coast of the U.S. to perhaps reposition to the Caribbean after passing through the Panama Canal. Another distinctive area to consider is Chinatown. Many years ago, I had a Chinese cooking class instructor who said there is no good Chinese food between Vancouver and San Francisco. The instructor's point was perhaps an inscrutable one since it is so obvious that western Canada and the U.S. west coast are notable for excellent Chinese food and large numbers of Asian and non-Asian consumers as well.

Caribbean Destinations

The Gulf of Mexico, Caribbean, and Atlantic Ocean in the region offshore from Florida, north of South America, and west of Mexico and Central America has an idyllic climate for tropical vacation islands and coastal resorts. It also has periodic hurricanes that are a concern for travelers, but they tend to be most prevalent during the hottest months from June through November, and their course and intensity is increasingly predictable. Predictions are so good that cruise ships simply alter their course as needed. The attractions of this region as a vacation destination are so great that it has become a preferred playground, and a slice of paradise, for millions of visitors each year. The distinctiveness of each specific destination often speaks for itself and makes it possible to go back again and again without retracing the same steps. The allure of the Caribbean is irresistible. Many of the best travel bargains to be found anywhere in the world can be found right there. My favorite personal experiences were the opportunities to swim with the dolphins and to be lifted out of the water by two dolphins swimming together, and going snorkeling in the clear tropical waters.

Cruise Ships

To date we have had the pleasure of completing approximately two dozen cruises and have typically enjoyed every minute of the experience. Once on board the all-inclusiveness and continual diversity of food, activities, entertainment, and excursions are unbeatable in my opinion as a comprehensive travel experience. We have never had an experience that we have regretted and have always come away with new acquaintances and friendships that are very much an addition to the new and exciting destinations. In a few words, the cruise ship itself is a distinct destination with virtually everything that a land-based resort can offer (well, maybe not horseback riding, except on a land excursion) and we only unpack once and let the experience roll. For a detailed review of all that cruise ships have to offer and ports of call, please see the constantly changing cruise reviews that are available on the Internet (e.g., www.cruisereviews.com, or www.portreviews.com), in travel magazines, and direct from each cruise line's website. If you have not experienced at least one cruise of at least one week in duration, you owe it to yourself to find out exactly what it is that makes cruising such a complete and enriching experience. Cruising can be the perfect vacation and the proof is in the number of people who repeat the cruise experience.

28
Travel Customs

Tourists don't know where they've been,
travellers don't know where they're going.
—Paul Theroux

The Private Car Remains the Vehicle of Choice

Most travelers still rely on their personal motor vehicle as the primary mode of transportation for leisure travel. The many benefits and typical cost savings are obvious for short trips, but not so obvious when a long distance is involved. Also, many people feel strongly that they are safer in a personal vehicle than on an airplane, train, or ship. It is true that the rate of private vehicle accidents per million miles driven has consistently improved over the years with better highway engineering design and safety improvements on many vehicles. However, the accident rate for cars is still quite high and continues to be impacted by drivers who fall asleep at the wheel, who do not adjust well to changes in driving conditions, or who  drive while drunk (especially when also angry). These same factors are not typical of commercial airline pilots, railroad engineers, or cruise ship captains, and their far lower accident rate per million miles traveled shows it every time. "One British study shows that flying is 15 times safer than car travel, 176 times safer than walking, and 300 times safer than riding a motorcycle." (Source: *BBC*

211

Health, May, 2001) It is customary, however, for most people to feel more in control when driving a private vehicle.

Tourism Is the World's Fastest-Growing Industry

Internationally, leisure travel now represents the world's largest civilian industry. Most of the world's countries with favorable weather conditions at least during a portion of each year have gravitated toward the hospitality and tourism industry in a very positive way. It is typically only in those areas plagued by warfare, civil war, rebellion, or terrorism that tourism is not yet an economic reality. For many travelers, the news reports from plagued areas will deter tourism for substantial periods of time and have major impacts on any new investment for tourist-friendly facilities in those areas. The economic logic is self-evident. Travel industry money flows to those nations that are perceived as safe.

To Improve Performance

Tipping, which literally evolved from the acronym meaning "to improve performance" (tip), began with roadside inns of Old England where service was notoriously deficient and provided by virtually unpaid, indentured servants, with little motivation to do

more than they were already obligated to do for their master. A plate or jar was typically set up on a counter where the travelers could place a coin to hopefully encourage some semblance of personal service during their stay. For some occupations the custom of tipping has become less and less discretionary and is often included as a fixed amount on the bill regardless of the quality of service of any one individual. The reality of much tipping is that many different service people contributed to the delivery of service received but are not at the immediate receiving end of what sometimes appears to be an "excess surcharge for minimum basic service."

Tipping may be the only source of cash income for service workers who are compensated only with room and board for long hours of service to others. Fiji, however, is one of the world's finest resort regions where tipping is usually not expected, and certainly not added to the bill. Japan and Singapore are additional areas where tipping is not the custom for hotels or taxis. In Vietnam, however, expect a 5 to 10 percent service charge to be added to your hotel bill and taxi drivers will gratefully accept any spare "dong" that you care to give them. Indonesia likewise adds a 5 to 10 percent service charge to the hotel bill to be divided among the entire staff. In most restaurants around the world, a minimum 10 to 15 percent gratuity is expected or is added as a service charge. U.S. travelers can generally expect to pay at least a one-dollar tip for each piece of luggage handled by a taxi driver, shuttle driver, or a bellhop. Leaving a tip each morning for the hotel maid is the most beneficial way to say thank you. A concierge, however, may be well-salaried but special requests should be preceded by a tip such as $20 in advance plus an additional tip on leaving if complex or detailed services were actually provided. A wine steward or restaurant maitre d' might also be tipped in advance or afterward if warranted by the circumstances.

Recently, on a Mississippi riverboat, this writer repeatedly observed a table of 10 people who were growing increasingly belligerent with the assistant waiter's slow service. At one point, the dining room manager even brought complimentary wine to the table. The very demanding group departed on the last night without paying any gratuity to the assistant waiter. The result was that he, a big fellow, was virtually in tears as he received no income for the entire week from that very difficult table. The reason he was slow, according to the dining room manager, was due to filling in for one or more persons in the kitchen because of staffing shortages. The dining room manager did not want to lose the employee so he paid the assistant waiter's tip out of his own pocket.

Local Law Takes Precedence
Local laws of the land must be respected wherever you are. Example: Where driving is done on the left-hand side of the road,

a common error is to suddenly find yourself on the "wrong" side of the road after making a turn. The consequences can be quite severe. In Belize, however, which was once British Honduras, the local law was to drive on the left-hand side of the road. But after achieving independence from the U.K., the local people ultimately switched the driving pattern to the right-hand side of the road out of respect for their neighbors in Guatemala and the Yucatan Peninsula of Mexico who already drove on the right. Encouraging all of the world's people to drive on the same side of the road is much like trying to get all Americans to accept the metric system of measurement, or to get all Europeans on the Euro.

Non-Verbal Communication Is Not the Same Everywhere

Gestures can and do have different meanings in different parts of the world. In Malaysia it is impolite to point with the index finger, but the same thing can be accomplished by pointing with the thumb. In India nodding the head means "no" and shaking the head means "yes." In Taiwan, the gesture for "no" is to raise your hand to the level of your face with the palm facing outward and wave that hand back and forth.

The mutual handshake with the right hand is becoming a pervasive custom throughout much of the world, but is still not the same everywhere. Originally, the handshake evolved as a signal of the intention to not hurt the person being greeted, and dates back to Roman army customs when the right hand might well conceal a dagger or the short Roman sword as an offensive weapon. In both Asia and the Middle-East, a handshake usually involves light grasping of the other's right hand, and tends to be limited to male-to-male exchanges only. In America and northern European nations, a handshake with a firm grip is a sign of strength and character, especially when accompanied with strong eye-to-eye contact as a further sign of interest and honesty. In Latin American countries women are almost as likely as the men to offer their right hand as an initial greeting. The following is a generalized summary of select variations:

• Japan

Initial greetings with westerners may involve a bow and a light grasp of the right hands with eyes averted to show politeness. Business cards (printed in both Japanese and English) tend to be offered  with both hands in such a way that they can be read by the receiver. Loud, boisterous, or demonstrative behavior is strictly avoided.

• Korea

Western and (South) Korean males tend to greet initially with a similar slight bow and light grasp of the right hand. Women tend to nod their acknowledgement as an initial greeting and avoid physical contact. If entering a private Korean home, it is polite to remove your shoes.

• China

Males now tend to shake hands as in Western cultures but demurely and perhaps after a slight bow. Like most of Asia, China has a long history of being a non-tactile culture with much ritualistic "stand-offishness." Silence, for example, is considered a sign of politeness, not rudeness. A smile can be a reflection of many emotions, or even a cover-up for embarrassment. Public displays of deep affection, pointing with fingers, and staring at others are avoided.

• Philippines

This nation of more than 1,000 islands and approximately 73 different language dialects is a much more tactile (sometimes called "touchy-feely") culture than most of Asia or the Middle East. There, it is considered rude to stare at anyone, or to speak loudly.

• U.S.A.

America is often described as a "melting pot" of cultures, but in general Americans tend to be non-tactile and concerned about any touching that might be considered rude, aggressive, or inappropriate. Shaking hands firmly or a light touch to another person's back or shoulder is about the extent of most publicly sanctioned touching. Unlike elevator and subway jamming situations in big cities of Asia, where comments are rare, it is impolite to bump into someone without saying "pardon me," or "excuse me." Personal space is readily sensed and looking at someone "straight in the eye" is considered interest and honesty, not rudeness or aggression.

- **Latin America**

Steady eye contact among Latino males can be taken as a sign of aggressiveness. Looking away tends to be a sign of respectfulness, not evasiveness. Physical space between people is closer in these expressive, tactile cultures than is comfortable for most Americans.

- **Middle East**

Persons of Muslim or Jewish faith are generally very sensitive about touching persons of the opposite gender in public. It is commonplace for two males to greet each other with a kiss to the cheek. Such greetings are also common in Brazil, France, and countries bordering the Mediterranean.

Cultural Distinctiveness

Learning another language involves far more than literal translations of one word for another. It includes all of the commonly understood expressions and a major sampling of another culture's values, philosophy, and customs. The non-verbal distinctions among different cultures are just one of the major components of communication that does not always translate one-on-one. Expressed in another way, people do attach different meanings to the same events. Consider a highly individualistic Australian (or American) who travels alone to a quiet and sunny beach within a collectivist culture such as Fiji, Tonga, Indonesia, Samoa, or many African nations. Soon, he is surrounded by large numbers of local people who ask endless questions and insist that he be included in their activities. In their minds, this must be a person of very low status who is in need of their assistance because he is traveling alone. It would never occur to them that he intentionally sought a quiet, peaceful, and isolated beach just to relax. The moral is simple. The exchange of communication would probably go much better if both sides had a better understanding of the other's culture and language. Nearly same behavior can produce very different results.

Consider a Limo

The impression is that chauffeured limousines are only for the rich and famous. Actually, there are a great many limo services that do cater to family or group transport to the airport at reasonable rates and there will be lots more space for the luggage than in a passenger car. The experience can make you feel like you are doing something special and memorable for that special occasion such as a major anniversary.

Expect Some Degree of the Unexpected

Most travel plans go as anticipated because they are carefully scheduled and involve many different people to help make everything proceed in a friendly and comfortable manner. There will still be those periodic occasions when something goes sour and must be dealt with quickly to avoid even more bizarre consequences. Often, it is these unanticipated and unplanned "glitches" that make the most interesting stories to share with others about your travel "adventures," not just a summary of everything that went exactly as planned.

Going Through Customs

Immigration offices do screening in just about every part of the world to enforce basic laws, to protect resident farmers and business people, and to screen for illegal substances. At times there can be real delays in getting through the process because a few people are holding up the system by doing things that are contrary to what is expected. Whenever in doubt you can and should contact the foreign consulate of the country you intend to visit to clarify what is legal and what may be illegal before entering that country and to confirm what you may be allowed to take out of that country and legally return to the U.S., Canada, or your home country. It can be exciting to bring back art "treasures," duty-free products, gemstones, and gifts for others legally and without concern that a particular customs limit may have been exceeded. Legally bringing back "bargains" is just one of the many inducements for vacation travel.

Our Fondest Memories Are Often Associated with Travel

Really great travel experiences are remembered for the rest of our days and a pleasure to share with other travelers when we don't tell the same story too often, or embellish it too much. The most memorable occasions tend to be a result of stretching our imagination and our budget to accomplish something that is special just for us. It does not have to be climbing the highest mountain, surviving in the wilderness, a honeymoon at the Taj Mahal, or circling the globe in record time. Great travel should be personally meaningful, exciting, and give you a great return on what you put into it. Great travel is not just another trip.

The trip to the hospital to be born is not a conscious memory for you as a newborn infant, but the travel required to get there at the right moment will be an indelible memory for your parents. Then, as you mature beyond childhood, one of the major accomplishments of your adolescence is to acquire a driver's license for the purpose of travel. More time will pass and in addition to all of life's little errands, travel will be associated with attending school, getting married, going to work, celebrating anniversaries, birthdays, vacations, and the significant moments of your life. Travel is very much a part of our lives from day one. Planned travel throughout the world can be a reality for you if you are determined to do it. In saying "Bon Voyage," or "Sayonara," or "Auf Wiedersehen," may your next vacation be heightened by the delight and joy of surprises that exceed your expectations. The adventures and out-of-the-ordinary memories acquired during a great vacation will remain with you—always.

Index

222